A TIMES BARTHOLOMEW GUIDE

HONG KONG SINGAPORE AND MACAU

Author: **Christine Routier-le Diraison**
Translation and additional text: **Gila Walker**
Editors: **Lisa Davidson-Petty, Alexandra Tufts-Simon**
Photo credits: **Ayer,** p. 42; **Evrard,** p. 107; **Jolivot,** pp. 59, 87; **Perier** (Explorer), p. 67; **Perno** (Explorer), pp. 31, 46; **De Selva** (Tapabor), pp. 35, 51, 79; **Singapore Tourist Board,** p. 115; **Straiton** (Explorer), pp. 12, 54-55; **Tovy,** p. 96; **Travert** (Hoa-Qui), pp. 111, 122, 127, 130, 135.

This edition published in Great Britain by **John Bartholomew & Son Ltd. Ducan Street, Edinburgh, EH9 ITA.**
This guide is adapted from *à Hong Kong, Macao, Singapour,* published by Hachette Guides Bleus, Paris, 1988.

© Hachette Guides Bleus, Paris, 1989. First edition.
English translation © Hachette Guides Bleus, Paris, 1989.
Maps © Hachette Guides Bleus, Paris, 1989.

British Library Cataloguing in Publication Data
Routier-le Diraison, Christine
  Hong Kong, Singapore & Macau. — (A Times Bartholomew guide)
  1. Hong Kong, 1843-1945: Visitors guides 2. Singapore:
Visitors guides 3. Macau: Visitors guides.
  I. Title II. à Hong Kong, Macao, Singapour. *English*
915.1'25044

  ISBN 0-7230-0324-6

Printed in France by Mame Imprimeurs (Tours)

A TIMES BARTHOLOMEW GUIDE

HONG KONG SINGAPORE AND MACAU

Published by
John Bartholomew & Son Ltd

HOW TO USE YOUR GUIDE

- Before you leave home, read the sections 'Planning Your Trip' pp. 9, 71, 93, 'Practical Information' pp. 13, 73, 97, 'In the Past' pp. 40, 81, 119 and 'Today' pp. 47, 84, 123 for Hong Kong, Macau and Singapore.

- The rest of the guide is for use once you arrive. It is divided into three sections: Hong Kong, Macau and Singapore. Each section includes practical information (accommodation, restaurants, tourist information, etc.) and itineraries with information on what to see.

- To quickly locate a site, a person or practical information, use the 'Index' p. 140. For further information concerning Hong Kong, Macau and Singapore, consult the 'Suggested Reading' section at the back of the guide.

- To easily locate recommended sites, hotels and restaurants on the maps, refer to the map coordinates printed in blue in the text. Example : Mandarin Hotel (C2).

SYMBOLS USED

Sites, monuments, museums, points of interest

***   Exceptional
**   Very interesting
*   Interesting

Hotels and restaurants

See pp. 13 and 25 for an explanation of hotel and restaurant categories.

MAPS

■ CONTENTS

INTRODUCTION TO HONG KONG

'**A** borrowed place, living on borrowed time'—this often-used expression describing Hong Kong was coined by journalist Richard Hughes and it fits Hong Kong to a tee. Ceded 'in perpetuity' by China to the British in 1842, the colony will revert to Chinese sovereignty on July 1, 1997. In the meantime, Hong Kong residents and foreign investors are scrambling to make the most out of the remaining years. This is Asia's busiest financial market, the third largest in the world, and the pace is frenetic. Nowhere is money made, or spent, as quickly.

Hong Kong is also a genuinely composite culture, a tantalizing and paradoxical place that leaves no visitor indifferent. Here, East meets West in this thriving capitalist enclave at the back door of the world's largest communist country. The city itself is certainly among the most modern in the world. During the day, skyscrapers and high-rise luxury apartments glitter against the skyline, while colourful neon signs, amid nightclubs, bars, restaurants and hotels, light the streets at night. Yet, barely hidden beneath its Western veneer, Chinese traditions live on, even in Central District, the business and shopping hub of the colony.

Deep in the winding side-streets, teeming with the mayhem typical of Chinese marketplaces, the air is filled with the clink of *mah-jongg* tiles and the smell of joss sticks burning in ancient temples. Outside the city, the New Territories include the mainland area to the north and the 235 outlying islands. There, in many of the rural settlements, villagers live as they have done for generations.

Everywhere, Chinese beliefs continue to guide daily life, and not only in the privacy of homes around the inevitable family altar. Hong Kong celebrates Chinese festivals, worships Chinese deities and observes rites of ancestor worship. Its residents believe that the principles of *fung shui* (wind-water), the correct alignment of the forces of nature, govern all aspects of life. Not a grave is dug, road laid or building constructed without first consulting a geomancer, an expert in *fung shui,* to determine its location and layout. Eight-sided mirrors are hung from windows to ward off evil spirits and certain numbers or sites are considered dangerous. Overlooking water (and when this isn't possible, an aquarium substitutes inside) is supposed to be auspicious. All these and a host of other beliefs are taken seriously by industrialists, high-finance managers and workers alike.

The visitor to Hong Kong can delight in this intoxicating territory without ever getting below the surface. Many of Hong Kong's five million annual tourists come here to take advantage of what has often been described as a shopper's paradise. An international free port, Hong Kong offers a multitude of goods at unbeatable prices (25-50% cheaper than in their country of origin). It is also a gourmet's delight: among its 19,000 dining establishments are some of the world's greatest restaurants, serving cuisines from the four corners of the earth, although Chinese cooking is undoubtedly the most outstanding. To further satisfy the epicurean, Hong Kong has some of the world's most outstanding hotels, providing unmatched service and comfort.

Why not start your visit with a 10-minute ride across the magnificent harbour, one of the busiest in the world? High-speed jetfoils carry passengers to Macau casinos; ferries ply between Hong Kong Island and Kowloon; luxury liners, cargo freighters and old Chinese junks and sampans float against a backdrop of skyscrapers, slums, luxury villas and squatters' huts: an eye-opening prelude to your stay in Hong Kong.

Hong Kong in brief

Location: Hong Kong lies at the south-east tip of China, 75 mi/120 km from Canton, just south of the Tropic of Cancer.

Area: 413.5 sq mi/1071 sq km. This includes the island of Hong Kong, Kowloon peninsula, the New Territories, the 235 outlying islands and Stonecutters Island.

Population: 5,681,300 inhabitants, of which 98% are Chinese.

Capital: Victoria on the island of Hong Kong is the administrative capital, but 40% of the population live on Kowloon.

Religion: Buddhism, Taoism and Confucianism are the three major religions.

Language: Chinese and English are the official languages. Cantonese is the most widely spoken Chinese dialect.

Political status: Hong Kong has been a British crown colony since 1842. According to the 1984 Sino-British agreement (see p. 45), all of Hong Kong will revert to China in 1997, while preserving a special status for at least 50 years.

Economic activity: Manufacturing of electrical and electronic equipment, textiles and clothing; trade-related activities; banking; hotels and restaurants.

PLANNING YOUR TRIP

▬▬ WHEN TO GO

The best time to visit Hong Kong is between October and December. These are the mildest and dryest months. Temperatures average 73° F/23° C with little difference between day- and night-time temperatures. From May to the end of September is monsoon season. Originating in the north-east, monsoons can bring scorching heat waves, torrential downpours and typhoons. January and February are the coldest months with an average temperature of 60° F/16° C and strong gusts of wind from the north. The weather is variable in March and April.

Average temperatures

	Jan	Feb	Mar	Apr	May	June	July	Aug	Sept	Oct	Nov	Dec
°F	58	59	64	71	79	81	84	83	81	76	69	62
°C	15	16	18	22	26	27	29	28	27	25	21	17

▬▬ GETTING THERE

Plane

More than 30 international airlines link Hong Kong to major cities around the world, including Air Canada, Air New Zealand, American Airlines, British Airways, Japan Air Lines, Philippine Airlines, Singapore Airlines, Thai Airways International, TWA and United Airlines. Many of these companies have offices in major cities in Australia, Canada, Great Britain and the United States. You can call them directly or contact your travel agent for further information concerning flights and organized tours.

The arrival at **Kai Tak Airport** is one of the most impressive in the world. Your plane will swoop down, brushing over tall buildings to land on a runway built out into the sea. The airport is located on Kowloon Peninsula, about 15 minutes from the Star Ferry, which crosses the harbour between Tsim Sha Tsui on the southern tip of Kowloon and Central District on Hong Kong Island. Most hotels provide limousine service from the airport.

If you are going to Hong Kong Island, you can take a taxi. In addition to the fare on the metre (approximately HK$25-30 to Kowloon, up to HK$60 for Hong Kong Island), you will have to pay a tunnel charge of HK$20 to cross the bay. It is cheaper to take a taxi to the Star Ferry and then another taxi when you arrive on Hong Kong Island, although this solution can be inconvenient if you have a lot of luggage.

Three buses link the airport to the city: the A1 goes to Tsim Sha Tsui and costs HK$6; the A2 goes to the Macau Ferry Terminal, Central District, Hong Kong, and costs HK$8; the A3 goes to Causeway Bay and costs HK$8.

Ship

Only 4.4% of visitors use this form of transportation to get to Hong Kong. If, however, the experience appeals to you, there are several possibilities, especially from other important Asian ports such as Singapore, Tokyo, Taipei, Canton and Shanghai. Among companies operating in the region are **American President Lines** and **Pacific & Orient**. For further details, contact your travel agent.

ENTRY FORMALITIES

Passport and visa

You must be in possession of a valid passport to travel to Hong Kong. If you are an American citizen, you can enter Hong Kong without a visa if you are going to stay for less than a month. If you are a Canadian or Australian citizen, you can enter without a visa for a stay of less than three months. British citizens can stay up to six months without a visa.

Travel to China

It is now possible to go to China from Hong Kong without applying to your embassy or consulate. You can procure a visa either from the **Chinese Embassy,** Visa Office of the Ministry of Foreign Affairs, 5th floor Lower Block, 26 Harbour Rd., Wan Chai, Hong Kong, ☎ 5-744163 or from travel agents who operate tours to China. A list of recognized travel agents is available from the Hong Kong Tourist Association (see pp. 11, 37).

Vaccinations

No vaccinations are required unless you are coming from or have passed through a cholera-infected area up to 14 days before arrival.

Customs

You can bring almost anything into Hong Kong. The only restrictions apply to tobacco (no more than 200 cigarettes and 50 cigars), alcohol (no more than one litre) and perfume (60 ml). In any case, you will have nothing to gain from bringing your own supplies, everything is very reasonable in Hong Kong.

MONEY

The unit of currency is the Hong Kong dollar (HK$). The HK$ has been linked to the US dollar since October 1983 at a fixed rate of US$1 = HK$7.80 (£1 = HK$13.4). Currency rates are published daily in the two principal English-language newspapers (see p. 28). Notes are in denominations of HK$10, HK$20, HK$50, HK$100, HK$500 and HK$1000. Coins are 10 cents, 20 cents and 50 cents, HK$1, HK$2 and HK$5.

Travellers' checks and most credit cards are accepted everywhere. Often, however, you will pay less if you use cash.

Budget

Life in Hong Kong is relatively expensive for the visitor. You can live well, if not luxuriously, on the equivalent of US$85 to US$140 a day. You will have a hard time getting by on less than US$45 a day. Tourists spend a good deal more on shopping in Hong Kong than on anything else. According to statistics published by the **Hong Kong Tourist Association (HKTA),** the breakdown of visitor expenditures is as follows:

- shopping: 54.0%
- hotels: 28.6%
- meals: 9.0%
- entertainment: 2.2%
- excursions: 2.4%
- miscellaneous: 3.8%

WHAT TO TAKE

Clothing

If you are planning to visit Hong Kong between May and September, during the monsoon season, be sure to take along light clothing and an umbrella. A sweater is useful all year round, even during the hottest months, because buildings in Hong Kong are generally air-conditioned and can be chilly. In autumn, from September to December, a light jacket is recommended. In January and February, you will need woolen clothing and a coat, especially if you get cold easily.

Medicine

Hong Kong has excellent hospital facilities and many hotels have a doctor on the premises. There is no need to bring along any special medications other than a supply of anything that you are taking regularly.

You can buy medicine in pharmacies (open daily 10am-10pm), department stores and shopping centres.

Photographic material

Hong Kong, like Singapore, is one of the best places in the world to buy photographic equipment. All the major brands are available. You needn't bring a supply of film since you can buy what you need at low prices. Finally, if you are visiting during the monsoon season, you will need waterproof wrappings.

BEFORE YOU LEAVE: SOME USEFUL ADDRESSES

The **Hong Kong Tourist Association** is an extremely efficient and helpful organization that has many overseas offices, including the following:

Australia
National Australia Bank House, 20th floor, 255 George St., Sydney NSW 2000, ☎ (02) 251 2855.

Great Britain
4th floor, 125 Pall Mall, London SW1Y 5EA, ☎ (01) 930 4775.

United States
590 Fifth Ave., New York, NY 10036-4706, ☎ (212) 869 5008.
Suite 2323, 333 N. Michigan Ave., Chicago, IL 60601-3966, ☎ (312) 782 3872.
Suite 404, 360 Post St., San Francisco, CA 94108-1568, ☎ (415) 781 4582.
Suite 1220, 10940 Wilshire Blvd., Los Angeles, CA 90024, ☎ (213) 208 4582.

The **British Tourist Authority** will also offer helpful and friendly advice, at least until 1997. They have offices at the following addresses:

Australia
171 Clarence St., Sydney NSW 2000, ☎ (02) 29 8627.

Canada
Suite 600, 94 Cumberland St., Toronto ONT M5R 3N3, ☎ (416) 925 6326.

United States
40 W. 57th St., New York, NY 10019, ☎ (212) 581 4700.
John Hancock Center, Suite 3320, 875 N. Michigan Ave., Chicago, IL 60611, ☎ (312) 787 0490.
612 S. Flower St., Los Angeles, CA 90017, ☎ (213) 623 8196.
Plaza of the Americas, Suite 750, North Tower, Dallas, TX 75201, ☎ (214) 720 4040.

PRACTICAL INFORMATION

ACCOMMODATION

Hotels

Hotels in Hong Kong are plentiful, varied and generally of excellent quality. Several of Hong Kong's highest quality hotels are world famous for their unmatched luxury and service. If you want a view of the harbour, choose a hotel on the Kowloon side overlooking the island of Hong Kong. In the following selective listing, all hotels are air-conditioned and have private bathrooms. Prices given are for double rooms and do not include tax (add 10-15%).

Luxury hotels (▲▲▲▲)

These hotels are, without a doubt, among the best in the world. They are better described as super-luxurious and offer all kinds of special amenities including health clubs, business services and some of the best restaurants in the city. Price range is between HK$750 and HK$1750.

First-class hotels (▲▲▲)

The hotels in this category offer almost the same quality as the luxury hotels. All rooms have telephones, radios and colour televisions. Usually the hotels have their own swimming pools and shopping arcades. Price range is between HK$550 and HK$1300.

Moderately priced hotels (▲▲)

The hotels in this category provide the same kind of comfort as the first-class hotels but the service is less individualized. There is usually a television in each room, with several restaurants, bars and boutiques available. Price range is between HK$350 and HK$900.

Inexpensive hotels (▲)

The hotels in this category are suitable for those who are looking for a base for their outdoor activities and are not particularly concerned with a hotel's amenities. Keep in mind that you can take advantage of the restaurants, nightclubs and bars of the grander hotels without staying in them. All the hotels listed below are well-kept and clean. Price range is between HK$150 and HK$380.

Day or night, Peking Road in Kowloon offers a variety of entertainment possibilities.

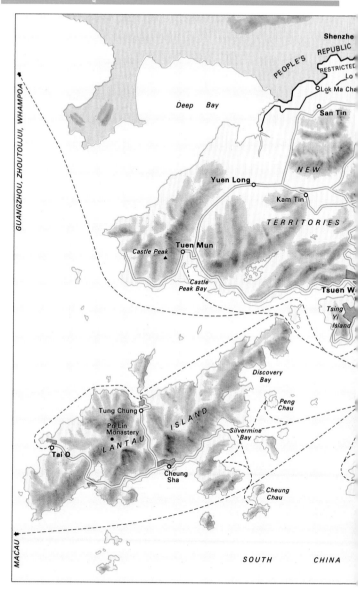

General map of Hong Kong and the New Territories.

Map coordinates refer to the map pp. 18-19, if in Hong Kong, and to the map pp. 20-21, if in Tsim Sha Tsui (Kowloon).

▲▲▲▲ **Mandarin Oriental,** 5 Connaught Rd., Hong Kong (C2), ☎ 5-220111, telex: 73653 MANDA HX. This prestigious hotel, at the foot of the Star Ferry on the Hong Kong side, offers fantastic service in a refined, superb setting. The construction of the Jardine House has cut it off from the bay but many rooms still have spectacular views. The hotel includes an enormous shopping centre, restaurants, bars (the favourite meeting place of Hong Kong high society), reception halls, a nightclub and more. 547 rooms.

▲▲▲▲ **Peninsula,** Salisbury Rd., Kowloon (B2), ☎ 3-666251, telex: 43821 PEN HX. Situated opposite the bay at the corner of Nathan and Salisbury roads, this is the favourite hotel of the international jet set. The overall atmosphere is formal, the rooms are immense, the lobby imposing and the service flawless. The hotel offers a sumptuous afternoon tea with a delicious selection of cakes—all you can eat for HK$70. 181 rooms.

▲▲▲▲ **Regal Meridien,** 71 Mody Rd., Tsim Sha Tsui East, Kowloon (D2), ☎ 3-7221818, telex: 40955 HOMRO HX. The Meridien re-creates a typically French atmosphere. You can dine in the luxurious **Restau-**

rant de France on the cuisine of Paul Bocuse, after sipping a Kir Royal at the **Rendezvous Bar.** 623 rooms.

▲▲▲▲ **Regent,** Salisbury Rd., Kowloon (C3)   ☎ 3-7211211, telex: 37134 REG HX. Anchored like a giant luxury liner, the Regent was built on land reclaimed from the sea opposite Hong Kong Island. It is worth a visit even if you cannot afford to stay here. Enormous bay windows allow you to take full advantage of the magnificent view. The architecture is imaginative and the decor refined. In spring, a field of chrysanthemums is planted in the lobby. 605 rooms.

▲▲▲▲ **Royal Garden,** 69 Mody Rd., Tsim Sha Tsui East, Kowloon (D2), ☎ 3-7215215, telex: 39539 RGHTL HX. The rooms here are very comfortable and the architecture surprising. The hotel is built around an extraordinary patio with a piano in the centre of a pond. 433 rooms.

▲▲▲▲ **Shangri-La,** 64 Mody Rd., Tsim Sha Tsui East, Kowloon (D2), ☎ 3-7212111, telex: 36718 SHALA HX. This prestigious hotel offers every imaginable luxury. 719 rooms.

▲▲▲ **Excelsior Hotel,** Causeway Bay, Hong Kong, ☎ 5-767365, telex: 74550 EXCON HX. An extremely comfortable hotel, the Excelsior has several restaurants (including a popular Italian restaurant), a theatre, a sauna, tennis courts and a shopping arcade. 923 rooms.

▲▲▲ **Furama Intercontinental,** 1 Connaught Rd., Hong Kong (D2), ☎ 5-255111, telex: 73081 FURAM HX. This 32-storey hotel is beautifully situated overlooking the bay from the Hong Kong side. Don't miss the marvelous view of all Hong Kong and Kowloon from its revolving restaurant. 522 rooms.

▲▲▲ **Golden Mile Holiday Inn,** 50 Nathan Rd., Kowloon (C2), ☎ 3-693111, telex: 56332 HOLIN ´HX. The usual comfort of the American chain is found here, topped off by quality Asian service. There is a pool on the top floor as well as three floors of restaurants, bars and boutiques. 577 rooms.

▲▲▲ **Hilton,** 2 Queen's Rd., Hong Kong (C3), ☎ 5-233111, telex: 73355 HILTL HX. Here you will find everything you'd expect from a Hilton hotel: a convenient location in the business district, a stunning view, great comfort and excellent service. The hotel offers its guests a cruise on the waters around Cheung Chau and Yau Ma Tei aboard the *Wang Fu,* a replica of a pirate ship from days gone by. 755 rooms.

▲▲▲ **Hyatt Regency,** 67 Nathan Rd., Kowloon (B2), ☎ 3-3111234, telex: 43127 HYATT HX. A five-minute walk from the Star Ferry, this hotel has a pleasant decor and includes a shopping arcade, restaurant, bar and nightclub. 723 rooms.

▲▲▲ **Lee Gardens,** Hysan Ave., Causeway Bay, Hong Kong, ☎ 5-9853311, telex: 75601 LEGAR HX. This hotel has European, Chinese and Japanese restaurants and offers attentive and efficient round-the-clock service. 800 rooms.

▲▲▲ **Miramar,** 130 Nathan Rd., Kowloon (C1), ☎ 3-681111, telex: 44661 MIRHO HX. Situated opposite Kowloon Park, the Miramar offers excellent service in a somewhat grandiose decor. 542 rooms.

▲▲▲ **Omni Hong Kong Hotel,** 3 Canton Rd., Kowloon (B2), ☎ 3-676011, telex: 43838 HONHO HX. Its location, in the Ocean Terminal commercial complex right outside the Star Ferry, provides a magnificent view over the harbour. 790 rooms.

▲▲▲ **Park Lane,** 310 Gloucester Rd., Causeway Bay, Hong Kong, ☎ 5-8903355, telex: 75343 PLH HX. Overlooking Victoria Park, it's a two-minute walk from the sampans at Causeway Bay Basin and houses a very good French restaurant. 850 rooms.

▲▲▲ **Sheraton,** 20 Nathan Rd., Kowloon (C2), ☎ 3-691111, telex: 45813 HKSHR HX. Situated at the beginning of Nathan Road, its view of the harbour has been spoiled by the recently constructed Tsim Sha Tsui East sector. There is still a splendid view from the rooftop pool and

Hong Kong Mass Transit Railway (MTR).

the **Sky Lounge** bar. There are 77 boutiques in its shopping arcade and numerous restaurants. 860 rooms.

▲▲▲ **Victoria,** 200 Connaught Rd., Hong Kong (B1), ☎ 5-407288, telex: 86608 HTLVT HX. This waterfront hotel is near the Macau Ferry Terminal. It has American, European and Cantonese restaurants and a swimming pool. 536 rooms.

▲▲ **Ambassador,** Nathan/Middle Rds., Kowloon (C2), ☎ 3-666321, telex: 43840 AMHOC HX. The rooms in this hotel, situated behind the Sheraton, are spacious. The restaurant on the top floor offers a good view of the harbour. 315 rooms.

▲▲ **Caravelle,** 84-86 Morrison Rd., Happy Valley, Hong Kong, ☎ 5-754455, telex: 65793 CARAV HX. At this comfortable hotel, you have your choice of American, Cantonese, French or Taiwanese cuisine. 102 rooms.

▲▲ **Empress,** 17-19 Chatham Rd., Kowloon (C2), ☎ 3-660211, telex: 44871 EMPTL HX. This high-rise hotel has American, Cantonese and Indonesian restaurants. 189 rooms.

▲▲ **Grand,** 14 Carnarvon Rd., Kowloon (C2), ☎ 3-669331, telex: 44838 GRAND HX. This charming hotel offers American and Cantonese cuisine, as well as a sumptuous Scandinavian smorgasbord. 194 rooms.

▲▲ **Imperial,** 32 Nathan Rd., Kowloon (C2), ☎ 3-662201, telex: 55893 IMPHO HX. This hotel has Chinese and Indonesian restaurants, a good view of the harbour and free airport transfer service. 300 rooms.

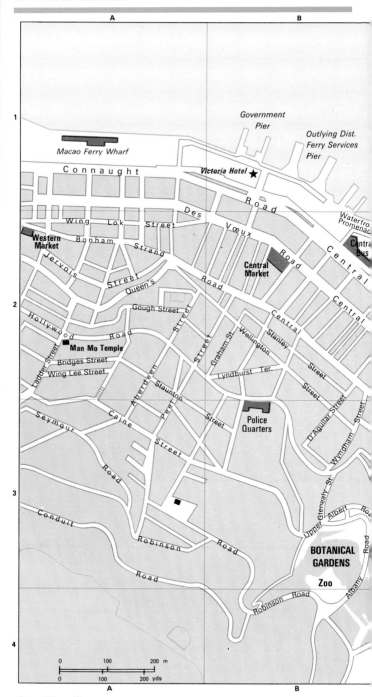

Central Hong Kong

■   Temple
▲   Shopping centre
★   Hotel

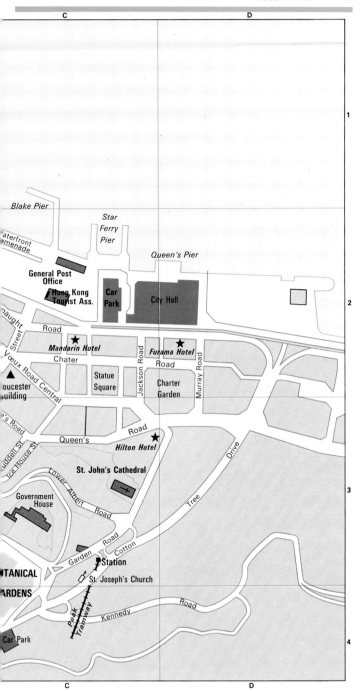

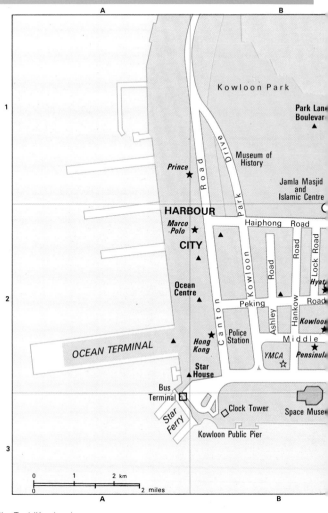

Tsim Sha Tsui (Kowloon)

★   Hotel   ○   MTR station
☆   Youth hostel   ▲   Shopping centre
■   Hong Kong Tourist Association

▲▲ **International,** 33 Cameron Rd., Kowloon (C2), ☎ 3-663381, telex: 34749 INTLH HX. This modern hotel offers Chinese and French cuisines. 89 rooms.

▲▲ **New World,** New World Centre, 22 Salisbury Rd., Kowloon (C3), ☎ 3-694111, telex: 35860 NWHTL HX. Hotel facilities include a swimming pool, a gym, shops and 24-hour service. 716 rooms.

▲▲ **Park,** 61-65 Chatham Rd., Kowloon (C1), ☎ 3-661371, telex: 45740 PARKH HX. This hotel is conveniently located in the centre of the commercial district. 410 rooms.

▲ **Bangkok Royal,** 2-12 Pilkem St., Yau Ma Tei, Kowloon, ☎ 3-679181. Modest but adequate, this hotel offers American, Cantonese and Thai cuisines. 70 rooms.

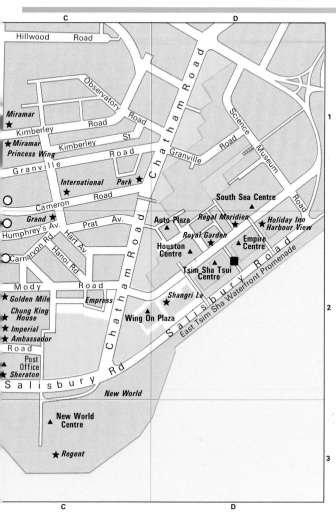

▲ **Fortuna,** 355 Nathan Rd., Kowloon (B1), ☎ 3-851011. This hotel has pleasantly decorated rooms and a restaurant offering American and Cantonese cuisines. 186 rooms.

▲ **Harbour,** 116-122 Gloucester Rd., Hong Kong, ☎ 5-748211. This motel-style accommodation has a view over the harbour and sampans of Causeway Bay. 200 rooms.

▲ **Harbour View International House,** 4 Harbour Rd., Wan Chai, Hong Kong, ☎ 5-201111. A YMCA, the Harbour View has better service and a more modern setting than most hostels. Half of the rooms overlook the harbour. 320 rooms.

▲ **Hong Kong Cathay,** 17 Tung Lo Wan Rd., Causeway Bay, Hong Kong, ☎ 5-778211. This modern hotel has a restaurant offering American and Indonesian cuisines. 150 rooms.

▲ **King's,** 473 Nathan Rd., Kowloon (B1), ☎ 3-7801281. This hotel has up-to-date decor and a restaurant offering American, Cantonese and Thai cuisines. 72 rooms.

▲ **Nathan,** 378 Nathan Rd., Kowloon (B1), ☎ 3-885141. This hotel is modern and attractive, with a restaurant offering American and Cantonese cuisines. 185 rooms.

▲ **New Astor,** 11 Carnarvon Rd., Kowloon (C2), ☎ 3-667261. Located in a lively district of Kowloon, the Astor is comfortable and has a pleasant ambience. 148 rooms.

▲ **New Harbour,** 41 Hennessy Rd., Wan Chai, Hong Kong, ☎ 3-8611166. Lively atmosphere and an excellent Chinese restaurant with a view of Hennessy Road. 173 rooms.

▲ **Shamrock,** 223 Nathan Rd., Kowloon (B1), ☎ 3-662271. A large hotel, the Shamrock has a restaurant offering American, Cantonese and Malaysian cuisines. 150 rooms.

Guest houses

Hong Kong guest houses resemble the modest Chinese hotels found throughout Asia. If it doesn't bother you to be woken up at 3am by your neighbours, if you care little about your surroundings and if you don't mind service that is nonchalant or simply nonexistent, you can choose from the list that follows. Price range is between HK$100 and HK$370. Inquire about special weekly or monthly rates.

Chungking Mansions, 40 Nathan Rd., Kowloon (C2). Conveniently located near several of the big hotels at the beginning of Nathan Road, this building contains numerous guest houses on its 16 floors. The best way to make your choice is to explore it yourself. We recommend **Chungking House** (4th and 5th floors, ☎ 3-665362). Many of the others are not very inviting.

International Youth Accommodation Centre, Lock Rd., Tsim Sha Tsui, Kowloon, ☎ 3-663419.

The YMCA and YWCA offer comfortable accommodation at the following addresses:

YMCA, Salisbury Rd., Kowloon (B2), ☎ 3-692211. 136 rooms.

YMCA, 23 Waterloo Rd., Kowloon, ☎ 3-7719111. 267 rooms.

YWCA, 5 Man Fuk Rd., Waterloo Road Hill, Kowloon, ☎ 3-7139211. 146 rooms.

▬▬ *AIRLINES*

Aer Lingus, 18th floor, Euro Trade Centre, 13-14 Connaught Rd., Central, Hong Kong (BC2), ☎ 5-265877.

Air Canada, 1026 Prince's Bldg., Hong Kong (C2), ☎ 5-221001.

Air France, 2114 Alexandra House, Hong Kong; GO7 Hotel Regal Meridien, Kowloon (C2), ☎ 5-248145.

Air New Zealand, Swire House, Hong Kong (C2), ☎ 5-8841488.

American Airlines, Room 202, Caxton House, Duddell St., Central, Hong Kong (C3), ☎ 5-257081.

British Airways, 30th floor, Alexandra House, Hong Kong; 112 Royal Garden Hotel, Kowloon (C2), ☎ 5-8680303.

British Caledonian Airways, 15th floor, BCC House, 10 Queen's Rd., Central, Hong Kong (C3), ☎ 5-260062.

Continental, 46th floor, Hopewell Centre, 183 Queen's Rd. East, Hong Kong, ☎ 5-299011.

Delta, 18th floor, Euro Trade Centre, 13-14 Connaught Rd., Central, Hong Kong (BC2), ☎ 5-265875.

Eastern Airlines, 201 d'Aguilar Pl., 7 d'Aguilar St., Hong Kong (B3), ☎ 5-237065.

Japan Airways, Gloucester Tower, Hong Kong (C2); Harbour View Holiday Inn Lobby, Kowloon (D2), ☎ 5-230081.

Korean Air Lines, St George's Bldg., Hong Kong; Tsim Sha Tsui Centre, Kowloon (C2), ☎ 5-235177.

Philippine Airlines, East Ocean Centre, 98 Granville Rd., Kowloon (D1), ☎ 3-694521.

Qantas Airways, Swire House, Hong Kong (C2); Sheraton Hotel Lobby, Kowloon (C2), ☎ 5-242101.

Singapore Airlines, 115 Gloucester Tower, Hong Kong (C2); Wing On Plaza, Tsim Sha Tsui, Kowloon, ☎ 5-202223.

Thai Air International, Shop 122, World-Wide Plaza, Hong Kong (C2); Peninsula Hotel Arcade, Kowloon (B2), ☎ 5-295601.

TWA, 2205 Yardley Commercial Bldg., Hong Kong (A1), ☎ 5-413117.

United Airlines, 29th floor, Gloucester Tower, Hong Kong (C2); Empire Centre, Tsim Sha Tsui East, Kowloon (D2), ☎ 5-8104888.

BUSINESS HOURS

Banks are open Monday to Friday, 9am-4:30pm, Saturday 9am-12:30pm. Stores are generally open as follows:

Hong Kong Island, Central District: 10am-6pm.

Hong Kong Island, Causeway Bay and Wan Chai: 10am-9:30pm.

Kowloon, Tsim Sha Tsui, Yau Ma Tei, Mong Kok and the commercial areas: 10am-9pm.

Kowloon, Tsim Sha Tsui East: 10am-7:30pm.

Most stores are open seven days a week; some of the department stores are closed on Sunday. During the Chinese New Year, which falls sometime in January or February (depending on the lunar calendar), most administrative offices and stores close for two or three days.

CONSULATES

Australia, 23rd-24th floors, Harbour Centre, 25 Harbour Rd., Wan Chai, ☎ 5-731881; open Mon-Fri 9am-noon, 1-4pm.

Canada, 13th-14th floors, Exchange Square, Tower I, 8 Connaught Place, Hong Kong (C2), ☎ 5-8104321; open Mon-Fri 8:30-11am.

Great Britain, c/o HK Immigration Dept., Mirror Tower, 61 Mody Rd., East Tsim Sha Tsui, Kowloon (C2), ☎ 3-7333111; open Mon-Fri 8:30am-12:30pm, 1:30-5pm, Sat 9am-noon.

Ireland, 8th floor, Prince's Bldg., Central, Hong Kong (C2), ☎ 5-226022; open Mon-Fri 9am-12:30pm, 2:30-5pm.

United States, 26 Garden Rd., Central, Hong Kong (D2), ☎ 5-239011; open Mon-Fri 8:30-10:30am.

CURRENCY EXCHANGE

All currencies can be bought and sold in Hong Kong, although US dollars are the most common. Licensed money-changers offer the best exchange rate. They are easy to find in Central District on Hong Kong Island and in Tsim Sha Tsui, Kowloon (especially along Nathan Road). You can also change money and travellers' checks in banks, hotels and the larger stores. The exchange rate can vary slightly from place to place. Avoid purchasing anything with foreign currency, even US dollars. You will inevitably lose out on the exchange.

ELECTRICITY

Electricity in all the hotels is 200 volts. Razor outlets have transformers and most hotels will supply you with adaptors for other electrical appliances.

EMERGENCIES

Hong Kong has numerous well-equipped hospitals. For a complete listing of doctors and dentists in Hong Kong, look in the telephone directory under 'Physicians and Surgeons' and 'Dental Surgeons'. The two main hospitals are:

Queen Elizabeth Hospital, Wylie Rd., Kowloon, ☎ 3-7102111.

Queen Mary Hospital, Pokfulam Rd., Hong Kong, ☎ 5-8192111.

The following numbers can be useful in an emergency:

Ambulance (Hong Kong): 5-766555.

Ambulance (Kowloon): 3-7135555.

Ambulance (New Territories): 0-4937543.

Emergency: 999.

FESTIVALS AND PUBLIC HOLIDAYS

Hong Kong celebrates with equal enthusiasm the birthdays of Queen Elizabeth, Confucius and Buddha, as well as those of Tin Hau (goddess of the sea) and Lu Pan (the master builder). The Chinese festivals follow the lunar calendar, which you can pick up from the **Hong Kong Tourist Association** (see pp. 11, 37).

January and February

Chinese New Year: The beginning of the lunar year is marked by three days of festivities and gift-exchanging. Most stores are closed during this time. Fireworks, once an integral part of the New Year celebration, have been prohibited by the government but there is still an official 30-minute fireworks display. The best places to watch it are from the Star Ferry Pier on the Hong Kong side and the jetty in Tsim Sha Tsui, Kowloon. Closing the Chinese New Year, on the 15th day of the first moon, is the **Lantern Festival,** when, at nightfall, thousands of traditional lanterns are lit on homes, temples and restaurants. For the most impressive view of this event, go to Victoria Park on Hong Kong Island or Ko Shan Road on Kowloon.

March and April

Ching Ming: On this day, which marks the beginning of spring, families visit the graves of their ancestors. Paper money is burnt as an offering.

Tin Hau Festival: On March 23, fishermen celebrate the birthday of their patron-goddess, Tin Hau, at the Tai Miao Temple at Joss House Bay and other temples dedicated to Tin Hau. Junks are decorated and temples are enveloped in clouds of incense smoke. Lion and dragon dances are performed on the islands of Cheung Chau and Lantau and at Causeway Bay on Hong Kong Island.

May and June

Cheung Chau (Bun) Festival: This festival comprises four days of festive ceremonies, parades, Chinese opera and theatre performances beginning on the eighth day of the fourth moon. Towers made of buns are built on the island of Cheung Chau and, on the third evening, participants climb up the towers trying to get hold of a bun, which is supposed to bring good luck in the year to come.

Tuen Ng (Dragon Boat) Festival: This is undoubtedly Hong Kong's most colourful festival. Dragon boat races, with boats built and decorated for the occasion, are held at Aberdeen, Tai Po, Yau Ma Tei and Stanley on the fifth day on the fifth moon. Special tours to see it are organized by local travel agents and tour operators.

August and September

Yue Lan (Hungry Ghosts) Festival: According to Chinese tradition, the spirits of the dead leave purgatory on the 15th day of the eighth month to enjoy themselves for a day on earth. Lots of incense and paper money are burned on this colourful occasion. These offerings are said to appease the wandering spirits, or Hungry Ghosts (those people who died without a proper burial or without family).

Mid-autumn (Moon Cake) Festival: In mid-September, moon cakes are exchanged and eaten as a reminder of those used in the 14th century to hide the secret messages calling for an uprising against the Mongols. Children light multi-coloured cellophane lanterns. A good place to go to enjoy this festival, if you don't mind crowds, is Victoria Park on Hong Kong Island.

October

Chung Yeung Festival: Thousands of Chinese go up to the top of the Peak (forming an incredibly long line) to celebrate this festival on the ninth day of the ninth moon (October). The tradition recalls a Chinese legend; the moral being that the higher up you are, the less you risk drowning.

FOOD

The Chinese take cooking seriously. They like to eat and they like to eat well. Their cuisine is greatly appreciated by epicureans throughout the world. There are as many types of Chinese cuisine as there are provinces in China. It would be impossible to enumerate all the regional cuisines available in Hong Kong; Cantonese is the most widespread, followed by Pekinese, Szechuan, Shanghainese and Hakka. Restaurants offer an enormous variety of dishes: many menus can run up to 20 pages or more.

The Chinese traditionally don't eat three meals a day and, while urban life has begun to impose a more structured eating rhythm, you will find that people eat at any time of the day in Hong Kong.

The decor of restaurants in Hong Kong is not directly related to the quality of food served. You can eat extremely well in restaurants that seem relatively shabby. Avoid, however, the low-budget outdoor restaurants. They are not always sanitary and you might find yourself with a serious case of indigestion the next morning. Restaurants tend to be extremely noisy, like school cafeterias the day before school lets out for summer holidays.

When you sit down in a restaurant, you will be brought a burning hot or ice-cold towel to wipe your hands and face. It is customary to order at least as many dishes as there are guests. Tables are generally round. You take a portion from each dish in the centre and place it on your plate. Bones and other inedible items are placed beside the plate, leaving the tablecloth covered with stains by the end of the meal.

There is no reason you can't learn to eat with chopsticks. If you are a beginner, you might find that you need to use a spoon or your fingers for certain dishes, such as crab claws, which are particularly difficult to hold.

Map coordinates refer to the map pp. 18-19, if in Hong Kong, and to the map pp. 20-21, if in Tsim Sha Tsui (Kowloon).

Three price brackets are given for Hong Kong restaurants. These are guidelines only, as prices will obviously vary depending on what you order.

(E) Expensive   HK$200 and up
(M) Moderate   HK$100 to 200
(I) Inexpensive   HK$100 or less

Cantonese

It is said that a Cantonese cook can prepare two meals a day for a year without making the same dish twice. The food is often steamed in bamboo baskets. *Dim sum* is a Cantonese speciality served in the morning and at lunchtime. You choose from trolleys which are rolled from table to table with an enormous variety of delicacies.

Jade Garden (M), 4th floor, Star House, Harbour Village, Kowloon (A1), ☎ 3-226888. Taste the roast pork, 100-year-old eggs, thick porridges, chicken cooked in earthenware and lotus leaves. Open daily 11:30am-11:30pm.

Man Wah (E), Mandarin Oriental Hotel, Connaught Rd., Hong Kong (C2), ☎ 5-220111. Excellent food served in a sumptuous setting. Jackets and ties are required for dinner. Open daily noon-3pm,6:30-11pm.

Yung Kee (M), 34-40 Wellington St., Hong Kong (B2), ☎ 5-221624. Specialities include 100-year-old eggs (said to be the best in town), frogs' legs in a variety of sauces and snake soup. Open daily 11am-midnight.

Pekinese

Peking cooking is spicier than Cantonese. Specialities include barbecues and various recipes using duck. Noodles are used more than rice.

New American Restaurant (M), 177-179 Wan Chai Rd., Hong Kong, ☎ 5-750458. The name is misleading; traditional Peking-style food is served here. Open daily noon-11pm.

Peking Garden (I), Alexandra House, Des Vœux Rd., Hong Kong (B2), ☎ 5-266456. Popular with many Hong Kong residents, not least for its energetic noodle-maker who offers a 'floor show' around 8pm. This restaurant has other branches: Star House, Salisbury Rd., Kowloon (B2), ☎ 3-698211; Empire Centre, Mody Rd., Tsim Sha Tsui East, Kowloon (D2), ☎ 3-687879. Open daily 11:30am-3pm, 6-11:30pm.

Spring Deer Restaurant (M), 42 Mody Rd., Kowloon (C2), ☎ 3-1233673. Peking duck is the speciality here. Open daily 11am-11pm.

Shanghainese

Shanghainese cuisine is spicy and uses more oil than Peking or Cantonese food. Dishes are often cooked for a very long time. One speciality is fresh-water crab, which is served in the autumn.

Great Shanghai (I), 26-36 Prat Ave., Kowloon (C2), ☎ 3-668158. Famous for its chicken dishes, but the braised turtle is also worth trying. The restaurant is lively and the prices are reasonable. Open daily 11am-midnight.

Sanno (M), 3 Cornwall Ave., Tsim Sha Tsui, Kowloon (C2), ☎ 3-671421. This is a comfortable, air-conditioned restaurant with delicious spiced beef and fresh-water crab. Open daily 11am-11pm.

Szechuan

Szechuan cooking is heavily spiced with garlic and hot pepper.

Lotus Pond (E), Harbour City, Canton Rd., Tsim Sha Tsui, Kowloon, ☎ 3-7241088. Try this elegant restaurant for its delicious garlic chicken. Open daily 11am-midnight.

Red Pepper (M), 7 Lan Fong Rd., Hong Kong, ☎ 5-768046. Its name is in keeping with the food served: braised beef in hot sauce, pepper soup, noodles in chili sauce, shrimp in garlic sauce. Open daily noon-midnight.

Western

The Chinese are as adept in the cooking and presentation of Western food as they are with Chinese food. Hong Kong offers a variety of excellent Western restaurants.

Amigo (E), 79 Wougneichung Rd., Happy Valley, Hong Kong, ☎ 5-772202. Located across the street from the race track, this French restaurant is a favorite with the local gourmets. Open daily noon-midnight.

Au Trou Normand (M), 6 Carnarvon Rd., Kowloon (C2), ☎ 3-668754. This is a highly reputed French restaurant, with specialities including crêpes Normandes and apple tarts. Open daily noon-11pm.

Gaddi's (E), Peninsula Hotel, Salisbury Rd., Kowloon (B2), ☎ 3-666251. Dress well for a deluxe dinner amid Colonial splendour. Open noon-3pm, 7pm-midnight.

Hugo's (M-E), Hyatt Regency Hotel, 67 Nathan Rd., Kowloon (B2), ☎ 3-662321. For a delicious, hearty roast beef, this is the place. Jacket and tie required for dinner. Open daily noon-3pm, 7-11pm.

Pierrot (E), Mandarin Oriental Hotel, Connaught Rd., Central, Hong Kong (C2), ☎ 5-220111. Rated one of the best French restaurants in the world; be sure to reserve in advance. Open Mon-Sat noon-3pm.

Plume (E), Regent Hotel, Salisbury Rd., Kowloon (B2), ☎ 3-7211211. Extremely elegant, with a stunning view of Hong Kong harbour, the Plume serves excellent nouvelle cuisine. Jacket and tie required. Open daily 7pm-2am.

If you hanker for a hamburger at a fast-food restaurant, Hong Kong has what you need. It has no less than 29 **McDonald's**, as well as **Kentucky Fried Chicken, Pizza Hut,** etc.

Hong Kong also has a wide range of restaurants offering cuisines from other Asian countries. You will find Korean barbecues, Japanese *tempura* and *sukiyaki*, Indonesian *satay*, Indian curry and so on.

Indian

Maharajah Restaurant (I), 222 Wan Chai Rd., Hong Kong, ☎ 5-749838. A wide variety of dishes from northern and southern India at unbeatable prices. Open daily noon-3pm, 6:30-11:30pm.

New Delhi (M), 52 Cameron Rd., Tsim Sha Tsui, Kowloon (C1), ☎ 3-664611. Specializes in northern Indian cuisine. Try the chicken and lamb curries, New Delhi style, and the tandoori. Open daily noon-2:30pm, 6:30-11pm.

Indonesian

Indonesian Restaurant (M), 26 Leighton Rd., Hong Kong, ☎ 5-779981. Excellent food served in simple setting. Try the rijstafel. Open daily noon-11pm.

Java Rijstafel (I), 1st floor, 38 Hankow Rd., Kowloon (B2), ☎ 3-671230. Open 11:30am-11pm.

Japanese

Benkay (M), The Landmark, Hong Kong (C2), ☎ 5-213344. Top quality Japanese cuisine in the heart of Central District. Open daily noon-3pm, 6pm-midnight.

Nadaman (M-E), Shangri-La Hotel, 64 Mody Rd., Kowloon (D2), ☎ 3-7212111. Traditional Japanese cuisine in small lovely restaurant. Reservations recommended. Open daily noon-3pm, 6:30-11pm.

Okahan (M-E), Lee Gardens Hotel, Hysan Ave., Causeway Bay, Hong Kong, ☎ 5-766188. Open daily noon-3pm, 7pm-midnight.

Unkai (E), Sheraton Hotel, Nathan Rd., Kowloon (C2), ☎ 3-691111. Open daily noon-3pm, 6:30pm-11pm.

Korean

Arirang Restaurant (M), Hyatt Regency Hotel, Nathan Rd., Kowloon (B2). Try the excellent barbecues. Open 11am-11pm.

Korea Restaurant (M), 56 Electric Rd., Hong Kong, ☎ 5-711731. Authentic Korean cooking. Try the beef or prawn barbecues.

Thai

Golden Elephant (M), Harbour City, Canton Rd., Kowloon (B2), ☎ 3-692733.

Sawadee Thai Restaurant (M), 1 Hillwood Rd., Kowloon, ☎ 3-725577.

Specialities include sour prawn soup and pineapple rice. Open 11:30am-11pm.

Floating restaurants

Don't miss eating excellent seafood on one of the three floating restaurants in Aberdeen (**Jumbo, ☎** 5-539111, **Sea Palace, ☎** 5-527340 or **Tai Pak, ☎** 5-525933; open 7am-11pm). Thousands of people still live on sampans in this fishing village which was once a pirate haunt. On the trip by sampan out to the floating restaurants (which are, in fact, as well anchored as the Jardine House), you will have a chance to enjoy the extraordinary sight of boats and junks in the harbour.

For an even more unusual experience, dine on a sampan at the typhoon shelters of Causeway Bay or Yau Ma Tei (April-October only). The sampan, which you can rent by the hour, is equipped with a sort of dining area (chairs, tables and dishware included). As soon as you leave the docks, you will be accosted by numerous small boats plying their wares (noodles, seafood, vegetables, drinks, etc.). Make your choice and watch as your meal is prepared in no time. From your sampan you will have an impressive view of the city lights. An added attraction is a floating orchestra which will perform Mandarin and Cantonese songs at your request. Restroom facilities on board are extremely primitive.

Dining with a view

Restaurants are often located on the top floors of the big hotels, adding the pleasure of a view to that of the palate. The sight of Hong Kong by night is truly enchanting. The two best restaurants of this kind are the **Furama Intercontinental** (D2; 1 Connaught Rd., Hong Kong, ☎ 5-255111) and **Juno Revolving Restaurant** (B2; 655 Nathan Rd., 26th floor, Kowloon, ☎ 3-915403). **The Eagle's Nest** (C3; 25th floor, Hilton Hotel, 2 Queen's Rd., Hong Kong, ☎ 5-233111) and **The Tower** (C4; Peak Tower Building, Upper Peak Tram Terminal, Victoria Peak, Hong Kong, ☎ 5-97260) also afford impressive views of the city. If you would like to enjoy the view over a drink, the **Sky Lounge** (C2; 18th floor, Sheraton Hotel, 20 Nathan Rd., Kowloon, ☎ 3-691111) offers one of the most stupendous vistas of Hong Kong and its harbour.

▬▬ LANGUAGE

The two official languages in Hong Kong are English and Cantonese. English is widely spoken, as it constitutes the only means of communication for those speaking different dialects. Cantonese, because it is a tonal dialect (with even more tones than Mandarin), is particularly difficult to learn.

Most signs are in English and English-speaking policemen have red badges on their uniforms.

▬▬ NEWSPAPERS

The two principal English-language newspapers are the *South China Morning Post* and the *Hong Kong Standard* (with morning and evening editions). They provide complete international news coverage. Other English-language dailies available in Hong Kong include the Asian edition of the *Wall Street Journal* and the *International Herald Tribune* (both printed in Hong Kong) and the official Chinese paper, *China Daily.*

The big hotels usually provide their guests with complimentary copies of the tourist weekly, *Orient,* and most of the English-language press.

▬▬ NIGHTLIFE

Few cities in the world can match the diversity of Hong Kong's night scene: the beauty of the harbour, the aggressive neon signs flashing in the dark, the feverish turbulence of markets that appear out of nowhere, the street operas, the clinking of *mah-jongg* tiles.

Bars

Like most ports, Hong Kong has a multitude of bars designed to furnish sailors with all that life on land can offer. The bars of Wan Chai on Hong Kong Island and around Nathan Road in Kowloon may have lost some of their former charm, but you can still drink in the company of friendly hostesses. There are also numerous topless places where the waitresses serve drinks from the inside of a circular bar. Customers pay extra for the pleasure of eyeing the almost naked waitresses while sipping cocktails.

Most of the big hotels have more sophisticated bars where you can enjoy your drinks in an elegant setting.

For a quiet drink

Chin Chin Bar, Hyatt Regency Hotel, 67 Nathan Rd., Kowloon (B2), ☎ 3-3111234. Open daily 11-2am.

The Jockey Pub, 108A Shopping Arcade, Swire House, Hong Kong (C2), ☎ 5-261478. Open Mon-Sat 11am-11pm.

Lookout Bar, top floor, Mandarin Oriental Hotel, Connaught Rd., Hong Kong (C2), ☎ 5-220111.

Sky Lounge, 18th floor, Sheraton Hotel, 20 Nathan Rd., Kowloon (C2), ☎ 3-691111.

Rick's Café, 4 Hart Ave., Kowloon (C2), ☎ 3-672939.

Hostess and topless bars

China City Nightclub, 67 Mody Rd., Kowloon (C2), ☎ 3-7231898. Open daily 6pm-3am.

Club Cabaret, New World Centre, Salisbury Rd., Kowloon (C3), ☎ 3-698431. Open daily 6pm-3am.

New Tonnochy Nightclub, 1 Tonnochy Rd., Hong Kong, ☎ 5-8931383. Open daily 6pm-3am.

Nightclubs and discos

Most hotels have their own nightclub or discotheque. Orchestras are usually Filipino and specialize in playing American hits. Among the hot spots at the hotels:

Eagle Nest, 25th floor, Hilton Hotel, 2 Queen's Rd., Hong Kong (C3), ☎ 5-233111. Open Sun-Thurs 10pm-1am, Fri and Sat 10pm-2am.

Pink Giraffe, Sheraton Hotel, 20 Nathan Rd., Kowloon (C2), ☎ 3-691111.

Other popular clubs include:

California, Lan Kwai Fong (off d'Aguilar St.), Hong Kong (B3), ☎ 5-211345. Open Mon, Tues and Thurs noon-1am, Wed, Fri and Sat noon-4am, Sun 5pm-1am.

Canton Disco, 19 Canton Rd., Kowloon (B2), ☎ 3-7210209. Open Sun-Thurs 9pm-3am, Fri and Sat 9pm-4am.

Nineteen 97, 9 Lan Kwai Fong, Hong Kong (B3), ☎ 5-260303. Open Mon-Thurs 10pm-4am, Fri and Sat 10pm-5am.

Chinese entertainment

Besides the usual activities, such as discos and nightclubs, that you can enjoy anywhere in the world, there are some purely Chinese forms of entertainment available in Hong Kong.

Cantonese cinema

Bruce Lee has come and gone (he died in 1973), but *kung fu* lives on in Hong Kong's film industry. Critics claim that the quality of martial arts films is not as impressive as it used to be, but a good storyline and big stars, such as Jackie Chan or Yuen Biao, can still attract crowds. Another popular genre is the new heroic gangster film, rich in gunfights, blood and gore.

Check the local newspapers for film programs. Evening showings are at 7:30pm, 9:30pm and sometimes at midnight. Seats cost between HK$23 and HK$26 and can be reserved two days in advance.

Cruises

Hong Kong Watertours (☎ 5-254808) operates daily cruises on motor-powered junks. Some daytime ferries become floating restaurants and nightclubs in the evening; with or without dinner, the romantic ambience is guaranteed. Departures are from Blake Pier, Connaught Rd., Hong Kong (B1) and Kowloon Pontoon near the Ocean Terminal. You can also take a sampan out on the harbour (see p. 37).

The **Star Ferry** schedules a one-hour harbour tour that is much simpler and cheaper than its competition. It leaves from Hong Kong and Kowloon Star Ferry terminals around 9:15am. The tour costs HK$110 and includes free drinks.

Night markets

These fantastic bazaars go up at nightfall, filling the most lifeless districts with bright lights and myriad sounds. The two better-known night markets are on **Temple Street** in Kowloon (go up Nathan Road, turn left on Jordan Road and then right on the third street) and the **Poor Man's Nightclub** (A1) near the Macau Ferry Terminal on Cleverly Street on Hong Kong Island. You can buy Chinese soups for HK$7, tailor-made shirts or cassettes of Cantonese hits (these cost only HK$42, but the quality of the recording is as low as its price). You can have your fortune told by a bird, pick up a strange remedy from among the extraordinary panoply of jars at any herbalist, and bargain for any number of other items.

Theatre restaurant

Rest assured, everything is Chinese here: the setting (vast dining room, bright lights), the cuisine (Cantonese, of course), the entertainment (elaborate) and the atmosphere (gregarious). Highly popular and recommended for having the most authentically 'Chinese' show: **Ocean Palace Restaurant and Nightclub,** 4 Ocean Centre, Kowloon (B2), ☎ 3-677111.

▬ ORGANIZING YOUR TIME

According to Hong Kong Tourist Association (HKTA) statistics, visitors spend, on the average, three-and-a-half days in Hong Kong. If they leave Hong Kong satisfied, it's because they don't known what they are missing. Contrary to popular belief, Hong Kong can be a destination in and of itself and not simply a shopping stopover.

Of the 235 islands of the colony, Cheung Chau, Lantau and Lamma are definitely worth a visit, or better still, an overnight stay. The New Territories, the fragile bridge between old and new China, are also interesting, offering a unique testimony to traditional Chinese life.

Hong Kong is an integral part of China today. It is most certainly not worth travelling thousands of miles just to go shopping. Hong Kong also provides a better understanding of one quarter of humanity if you only take the time to get to know it.

If you have only one week to spend in Hong Kong, we suggest that you spend two days in the islands and the rest in Hong Kong, Kowloon and the New Territories.

▬ POST OFFICE

The simplest way to send a letter or postcard is to leave it with the reception desk at your hotel. Many shopkeepers will send your purchases back home for you but don't expect them quickly; this service can take

A superb floral decoration announces the grand opening of a new store.

many months. Telegrams can be sent from hotels (10% service charge) or by telephoning Cable Wireless Phonogram (☎ 3-7324299).

The two main post offices are:

Hong Kong Central, 2 Connaught Pl. (C2), ☎ 5-231071.

Kowloon, 10 Middle Rd., Tsim Sha Tsui (C2), ☎ 3-66411.

They are open Monday to Saturday 8am-6pm. Other post offices are open the same hours except that on Saturday they are open 9am-1pm.

▬▬ SHOPPING

It sometimes seems as if Hong Kong were deliberately trying to induce you to spend your last cent. There is so much to buy that the visitor is likely to be torn between enthusiasm and sheer panic. Like Singapore, Hong Kong is a duty-free port and most goods are 25-50% cheaper than in their country of origin. One word of advice: before you set out on a shopping spree, put aside enough money for the taxi ride to the airport!

There are two basic systems of shopping: methodical and impulsive. Methodical shopping consists of canvassing a number of pre-selected stores handling a specific, usually expensive, item that you intend to purchase (diamonds, cameras, stereo equipment, etc.). *The Official Guide to Shopping, Eating Out and Services in Hong Kong,* published by the HKTA, is indispensable for the methodical shopper. It contains a complete list of HKTA-licensed shops by product category. Be ready to do a lot of walking on the streets around Nathan Road in Kowloon, as well as in the area between Central District and Causeway Bay on Hong Kong Island. Methodical shopping requires a robust constitution and a comfortable pair of shoes.

Impulsive shopping involves adventuring out, without a particular purchase in mind, and following your intuition. It is probably the best way to discover the specifically Asian character of Hong Kong commerce: its markets, herbalists, calligraphers, etc. The impulsive shopper, too, can make expensive purchases, if the necessary precautions are taken (see 'Bargaining' and 'Guarantees').

Try to visit one of the amazing shopping malls, if only for a few minutes' browsing. These large complexes offer dozens of shops under one roof, as well as shelter from the rain or heat. **The Landmark** (C2), conviently located in Central District, is the most prestigious, featuring big-name designer boutiques, cafés, a grocery store and a Pizza Hut. In Kowloon, explore **Ocean Terminal,** located right next to the Star Ferry Terminal. This vast mall offers everything from glorious antiques to toys.

Bargaining

Everybody bargains for everything in Hong Kong. The tone of negotiations tends to be calm, with each party trying to reach a suitable compromise. Take advantage of the competition among numerous shops selling the same products. Compare prices before making an important purchase and always try your luck by asking for a reduction, even in department stores.

Guarantees

Getting a guarantee in Hong Kong is no problem. Shopkeepers will happily supply you with all the guarantees you want. Unfortunately, once you're thousands of miles away, you might discover that it is of absolutely no value. Beware of guarantees that are valid only in Hong Kong. Other supposedly international guarantees can be worthless counterfeits. Buying important items only from HKTA-recommended dealers is one way to avoid being duped. Certain manufacturers deliver international guarantees only to their licensed distributors. Always check to see that the model and serial number on the guarantee correspond to the object purchased.

Warning

It is useless to try to outsmart customs officials with false receipts: they are perfectly aware of the prices in Hong Kong.

Antiques

Hong Kong is one of the best places in the world to buy Chinese antiques: porcelain, ceramics, ivory, jade, silk paintings, lacquerware, bronze, wood sculpture, furniture and more. Real antiques cannot be acquired at bargain prices: they are expensive and only a connoisseur can distinguish them from good, equally expensive, reproductions. Most ivory is artificially aged. Milky-coloured jade is extremely rare. More common is green jade, the jadeite of Burma. These distinctions can be made only by specialists using complex techniques. If you're not a connoisseur, your best bet is to purchase from a reputable dealer. The antique district is on **Cat Street** and **Hollywood Road** on Hong Kong Island (A2 see p. 57). Top-of-the-line items are also sold in the shopping complexes **(Star House, Ocean Terminal** in Tsim Sha Tsui, A2) and in the luxury hotels. A good place to see quality before hunting for bargains elsewhere is **Charlotte Hortsmann & Gerald Godfrey** (Ocean Terminal), a large up-scale bazaar with some of the best Oriental antiques.

Cameras

Most major brands are available in Hong Kong and, on the average, prices are 40% cheaper than you can find at home. Discounts on the suggested retail price can go up to 25%. Watch out, however, for bargains that seem too good to be true! Shop around and compare prices, in particular for accessories which can differ as much as 100% from store to store. Make sure the serial numbers on the camera body, the lenses and the accessories match. All major models are distributed by authorized dealers who will furnish you with a manufacturer's guarantee that is valid worldwide.

Chinoiseries

Hong Kong is a major outlet for products manufactured in China. Browse around in the Chinese emporiums for Chinese arts and crafts: silk items, jewelry, wickerware, porcelain, lacquerware, etc. You can't bargain in these shops but the prices are unbeatable. Some addresses:

Chung Kiu Chinese Products Emporium, 528-532 Nathan Rd., Kowloon (B1).

Yue Ha Chinese Products Emporium, 301-309 Nathan Rd., Kowloon (B1). This store has other branches at Park Lane Shoppers Blvd., 143-161 Nathan Rd. (C1), and Mirador Mansion, Kowloon (C2).

China Products Company, 488-500 Hennessy Rd., Causeway Bay, Hong Kong.

Chinese Merchandise Emporium, 92-104 Queen's Rd., Hong Kong (C3). This store has another branch at 65 Argyle St., Mong Kok, Kowloon.

Chinese Arts and Crafts, Star House, Kowloon (AB2). This store has another branch at Silvercord Plaza, Canton Rd., Kowloon (B2).

Clothing

Hong Kong tailors are reputed to be capable of creating a suit in 24 hours. If you want a quality product, though, you'd better give them at least five days. A wide selection of fabric from all over the world can be purchased here. Bring your material to the tailor with an illustration, a pattern, a model or simply your ideas. At least two fittings are recommended.

You can also buy furs, either ready-made or made-to-order, at very competitive prices.

Jewelry

An impressive variety of gems—pearls, rubies of Burma, sapphires, emeralds, zircons, diamonds, turquoises, topazes—all beautifully cut, mounted and set, fill Hong Kong jewelry shops. The prices are considerably lower than in other parts of the world, but don't expect miracles. The diamonds you'll come across here usually originate in Amsterdam or Antwerp, which accounts for the high prices. Before purchasing a diamond, contact the **Diamond Importers Association,** Room 1707, 17th floor, Lane Crawford House, 70 Queens Rd., Central Hong Kong (B2), ☎ 5-235497. It can furnish you with a list of its 38 members.

Opticians

Opticians, especially numerous in Hong Kong, sell a wide selection of frames and will fit them with suitable lenses (bifocal, tinted, etc.). Contact lenses, soft or hard, are moderately priced.

Radio, stereo, video equipment / electrical appliances

Numerous precautions should be taken before purchasing audiovisual equipment or electrical appliances. Check that voltage and frequency of current are the same as what you have at home. Clocks, for instance, will not keep the right time if the frequency doesn't correspond. Radios are not necessarily tuned to the same frequencies as those back home and broadcasting standards for televisions and video systems differ from country to country. When you buy equipment with several components, make sure the serial numbers agree. It may be difficult to get an exchange or refund later if there is a mistake, and you might not realize that your equipment doesn't work until you get home. By being informed and carefully questioning the salesman before making important purchases, you can avoid problems later.

Watches

This is another item that is plagued by counterfeiting. It is common to come across replicas of Cartier watches manufactured locally or Swiss watches with cheap Soviet movements inside.

Miscellaneous

Other interesting buys include perfume (Hermès, Chanel, Dior, Guerlain), lighters (Dupont, Dunhill, Ronson), baggage (made to your specifications), sports equipment, wigs, embroidered tablecloths, musical instruments and toys. They are all tax-free and you can always try bargaining for further reductions.

Unusual and inexpensive souvenirs

If you take the time to browse around while you're touring Hong Kong, you can pick up plenty of inexpensive souvenirs to take back home. Here are some gift ideas sure to delight your friends:

● *Who's Who of Communist China:* A biographical listing of all the powerful (or once powerful) figures of neighbouring China. At bookstores.

● Chinese horoscopes. In temples.

● Cassettes of traditional music (opera or music-hall): The quality of the recordings is mediocre but they cost only HK$42. At the Temple Street market.

● *Kung fu* teaching manuals. At bookstores.

● Chinese puzzles (otherwise known as a 'Chinese computer') with the solution included. In Chinese emporiums.

● Chinese calligraphy kits, complete with brush and ink stone. In Chinese emporiums in the school supplies department.

● Mickey Mouse electronic calculators for children. In stores selling electrical and electronic equipment.

● Magical potions (preferably labeled in Chinese) such as dried sea horse, tiger claws, rhinoceros horns, roots, mushrooms, etc. Their medicinal properties will astonish your friends back home, if they have the courage to try them. At herbalists in the Cat Street area.

● Chinese wine, such as 'green bamboo leaf', 'Mai Kuei Loh' or rice

Modern Hong Kong overlooks the floating city of sampans in the harbour.

alcohol. It is said that the best wines are those in which serpents were marinated. At wine shops in the Cat Street area.

SIGHTSEEING TOURS

There are several dozen organized tours offered by the HKTA and private companies that explore Hong Kong and the surrounding islands. Information and reservations are available at most hotels and the HKTA can provide brochures for further information. The list below briefly describes the most popular excursions in and around Hong Kong.

Hong Kong Island Tour

This three- or four-hour tour departs daily from all the major hotels. The route varies, but always includes a trip to Victoria Peak for a panoramic view of the city. Other sites generally included are Repulse Bay, Deep Water Bay and Shek O, on the south and east coasts of Hong Kong Island, the Stanley market, and Aberdeen. The tour costs HK$80 by coach and HK$450 by private car (maximum four people).

The Land and Water Tours

Water Tours of Hong Kong Ltd. and the **Seaview Harbour Tour Company Ltd.** offer a wide selection of tours by junk or cruiser. The simplest is a one- or two-hour cruise of the harbour; the most elaborate includes dinner and a trip to one of the islands. Ask at your hotel or contact the HKTA for prices of specific tours.

The Land Between Tour

This six-hour tour provides a fascinating glimpse into rural Hong Kong and the New Territories. For HK$180, you visit Tai Mo Shan, Hong Kong's highest mountain, and the Luen Wo market in Fanling. The tour returns via Plover Cove, where lunch is provided, and ends with a trip to the famous Sha Tin racecourse.

Ocean Park (see p. 60)

This is the largest amusement park and aquarium in the Far East. A half-day tour, which costs HK$170 for adults and HK$130 for children, includes all rides, the giant aquarium and the Ocean Theatre. The highlight of the marineland is the exceptional dolphin and killer whale show.

Sung Dynasty Village (see p. 62)

An entire 1000-year old Chinese village has been re-created, complete with period costumes, craftsmen and traditional shops. The three-hour tour includes either a snack, lunch or dinner and costs HK$145-190 for adults and HK$105-128 for children.

▅▅ SPORTS

Hong Kong hosts numerous athletic competitions, including the Hong Kong Open golf championship, the Coast of China Marathon, a windsurfing regatta, a Rugby Sevens competition, the Seiko Super Tennis Classic and the biennial China Sea Race between Hong Kong and the Philippines. There are two racetracks, at Happy Valley on Hong Kong Island and at Sha Tin in the New Territories. Races are held on Wednesday nights, Saturday afternoons (and some Sundays) from September to May. Tourists can go to the races as guests of the **Royal Hong Kong Jockey Club** or on a special HKTA tour.

You can also practice just about any sport you'd like in Hong Kong. Contact the HKTA (☎ 3-7225555) for further information concerning fees and equipment rental.

Golf

On weekdays, visitors can play golf at the **Royal Hong Kong Golf Club's** excellent courses at Fanling in the New Territories and at Deep Water Bay on Hong Kong Island. Call in advance for reservations (Fanling, ☎ 0-901211; Deep Water Bay, ☎ 5-8127070). **Discovery Bay Golf Club** (☎ 5-9877271) is open seven days a week to visitors. It is also possible to use the facilities at the **Clearwater Bay Golf and Country Club** by going on a special tour organized by the HKTA.

Hiking

There are 21 protected country parks with footpaths covering 173 mi/277 km. The best are the two on Lantau Island and the MacLehose Trail (named after the former governor) in the New Territories. Extensive information and maps are available from **Hong Kong Government Publications,** in the General Post Office Building in central Hong Kong (C2).

Martial arts

Every morning between 6 and 8am, Hong Kong witnesses an unusual ritual. In every park and in each open space, people, in a state of utmost concentration, are performing a sort of slow-motion dance. *Tai chi,* or shadow boxing, is of Taoist origin. Used to develop the concentration of the mind and the control of the body, it is made up of hundreds of movements with poetic names such as 'grasping the bird's tail', 'playing the violin' or 'pushing away the monkey'. Each exercise is associated with a mental image. You can observe the practitioners of this martial art, mostly women and the elderly, at Kowloon Park, Victoria Park or the Botanical Gardens. Hong Kong has become the capital of *kung fu,* a martial art invented by Buddhist monks in the 5th century. Most Chinese, especially the young, can go on for hours about the virtues of the different styles of *kung fu.* Numerous institutions teach the art of *kung fu* but they are generally open only to the initiated. Knowledge of Chinese is required and the training is as exacting spiritually as it is physically. If you are interested, contact the **Hong Kong Chinese Martial Art Association,** 687 Nathan Rd., Kowloon (B1), ☎ 3-944803. One of the most well-known schools sometimes opens its doors to spectators: **Luk Chi Fu School,** 446 Hennessy Rd., Hong Kong, ☎ 5-8911044.

Tennis

There are numerous courts in Hong Kong's sports centres but they are crowded and it can be difficult to reserve one. The cost of a court ranges from HK$15-30 per hour, depending on the time of day. Call any of the following centres before setting off with your tennis racket: **Victoria Park,** Causeway Bay, Hong Kong, open 7am-11pm, ☎ 5-706186; **King's Park,** Kowloon, ☎ 3-858985; **Tennis Centre,** Wong Nei Chung Rd., Hong Kong, open 7am-11pm, ☎ 5-749122; or **Jubilee Sports Centre,** Sha Tin, ☎ 0-6051212.

Water-sports

You can rent a junk, with or without a crew, through the **Boating Centre,** Edko Tower, 32 Ice House St., Hong Kong (C3), ☎ 5-223527. Sampans can be rented at Aberdeen or at the Causeway Bay or Yaumati typhoon shelters. If you belong to a yacht club, the **Royal Hong Kong Yacht Club,** Kellett Island, Causeway Bay, Hong Kong, has reciprocal arrangements with many international clubs (for information, ☎ 5-8325972).

Visitors can water-ski at Deep Water Bay on the south of Hong Kong Island. For information, call the **Deep Water Bay Speedboat Company,** ☎ 5-8120390. There are wind-surfing centres, where you can rent equipment or take lessons. The best are located at **Stanley Beach,** Hong Kong Island, ☎ 5-660320; **Tung Wan Beach,** Cheung Chau Island, ☎ 5-9818316; and **Tolo Harbour,** New Territories, ☎ 0-6582888. For information on beaches, see p. 60.

TELEPHONE

The telephone system is reliable and local calls are free from most restaurants and shops. Public telephone booths work with HK$1 coins. Telephone numbers are preceded by area codes: **5** for Hong Kong Island and the surrounding islands, **3** for Kowloon Peninsula and **0** for the New Territories. Use the area codes only when calling from one area to another.

For operator-assisted long-distance calls, dial **010** from your hotel; for directory information, **108.** You can call directly from one of the **Cable and Wireless** offices. The main offices, open 24 hours, are in Exchange Square, Connaught Centre, Hong Kong; Hermes House, Middle Road, Tsim Sha Tsui, Kowloon; and New Mercury House, Fenwick Street, Wan Chai. A three-minute call (minimum) to the United States, Canada and Australia costs HK$63; to Great Britain HK$60.

TIME

Hong Kong local time is GMT + 8, which means that it is eight hours ahead of London, 13 hours ahead of New York and 16 hours ahead of Los Angeles. Add another hour in the summer (from the end of April to the end of October).

TIPPING

Most hotels and restaurants include a 10% service charge on your bill but you can always leave a bit more if the service has been particularly good.

TOURIST INFORMATION

The **Hong Kong Tourist Association (HKTA)** is extremely active in promoting tourism. It publishes numerous brochures (transportation, walking tours, etc.) that visitors will find particularly useful. Hotel rooms usually provide courtesy copies of an HKTA mini-guide, jam-packed with useful addresses and practical information.

You will find a friendly and helpful welcome at the HKTA main office, 35th floor, Jardine House, Hong Kong {C2}, ☎ 5-244191. HKTA also has a counter at the airport and offices at the Star Ferry Terminal of Kowloon and the Royal Garden Hotel.

Some useful telephone numbers:

Airport: 3-769753.

Emergency Assistance: 999.

HKTA Tourist Association Visitor Hotline: 3-7225555.

Police Hot Line: 5-277177.

Time and Temperature: 5-1152.

Tourist Assistance: 3-671111.

▬▬ TRANSPORTATION

It won't take you long to find your way around Hong Kong, especially in Kowloon, where the streets generally run from north to south and from east to west. You can obtain a street map of Hong Kong Island and Kowloon from the **HKTA** (see p. 37). All street names are indicated in English and the transportation system is excellent. If you need assistance from a policeman, those with red badges on their shoulders speak English.

Bus

This is an extremely economical means of transportation, costing between HK$1.5 and HK$5.4 in the city (you must have exact change). Buses run from 6am-midnight. The routes are indicated at the main stations but not at the smaller stops; final destinations are marked on the bus. Avoid taking the bus on weekends, holidays and during peak hours (8-9:30am, 12:30-2:30pm, 4-6:30pm). You can get a copy of the HKTA *Official Guide Book* if you want to do your sightseeing by bus.

Ferry

The **Star Ferry** (C2) operates from 6:30am-11:30pm between Central District, Hong Kong Island, and Tsim Sha Tsui on Kowloon, and from 7am-7pm between Central District and Hung Hom (the terminal for the trains to the New Territories and China). The Star Ferry used to be the principal link between Hong Kong Island and Kowloon until the subway (MTR) was built. It remains a classic symbol of Hong Kong and offers a scenic trip across the harbour for a mere HK80 cents in first class or HK50 cents in second. The ride to Hung Hom costs HK80 cents. The **Hong Kong Ferry Company** links Central District, Hong Kong Island, with Yau Ma Tei on Kowloon, with further service to Mong Kok, Sham Shui Po and Tai Kok Tsin. The ferries to the nearby islands leave principally from Connaught Road in central Hong Kong   ).   (A1)

Mass Transit Railway (MTR)

The MTR, with 14 stops on the island and 23 on Kowloon, is one of the quickest ways of getting around (see map p. 17). It runs from 5am-1am and is extremely easy to use. Tickets, in the form of magnetic cards resembling credit cards, cost between HK$2.50 and HK$6, depending on the distance travelled, and can be purchased from vending machines. You can obtain small change from change machines.

A **Tourist Ticket** can be bought at HKTA offices and in all MTR stations. It costs HK$20, remains valid for several trips and can also be used on the Kowloon-Canton railway.

Minibus

These small (14 seats) yellow buses with red stripes are similar to collective taxis. They run set routes, but will stop anywhere along the way to pick up or drop off passengers. Fares range between HK$2 and HK$6, depending on distance, weather conditions (a sort of 'rain tax') and traffic. Visitors will find the use of minibuses difficult since their itineraries are not indicated but if you want to try them out, go to the main terminals near the Connaught Centre in central Hong Kong (C2), or at the Jordan Road Ferry Pier in Kowloon.

Rickshaw

Although the government stopped issuing rickshaw licenses many years ago, a few survivors of this improbable means of transportation remain. You can find them mostly at the entrance to the Star Ferry on the Hong Kong side. These elderly pullers with muscular legs spend much of the day seated by their rickshaws. Residents sometimes hire them to transport packages or persons. Fares, calculated on the basis of about HK$50 for five minutes, must be negotiated in advance.

Taxi

Taxis are plentiful on Hong Kong Island and Kowloon, though they can be hard to find during rush hour or when it's raining. A taxi is available when its light is on. Most drivers speak English and fares are indicated on the metre (HK$6.5 for the first 1.2 mi/2 km). Remember that there is a HK$20 tunnel surcharge when crossing the harbour and a surcharge of HK$2 per large piece of luggage.

Some average fares:

From the Star Ferry on the Hong Kong side to Victoria Peak costs HK$29, to Aberdeen HK$37, to Repulse Bay HK$40, to Tiger Balm Garden HK$29.

From the Star Ferry on the Kowloon side to Kai Tak Airport costs HK$20, to Lai Chi Kok HK$29, to Sha Tin HK$52, to Tai Po HK$64.

Train

Hung Hom Station, a 20-minute walk from Tsim Sha Tsui or a Star Ferry ride from Central District, is the terminal of the efficient Kowloon-Canton Railroad. Frequent commuter trains run from here into the New Territories and there are four daily non-stop express trains to Canton (from where connections can be made to major cities in China). The train runs through Kowloon, Sha Tin and along scenic Tolo Harbour. Holders of Chinese visas can get off the commuter train at Sheung Shui (18.75 mi/30 km, or about 20 minutes from Hung Hom) and walk across the border into the booming Chinese special economic zone of Shenzhen. The Kowloon-Canton Railroad also connects with the Mass Transit Railway at Kowloon Tong station.

Kowloon-Canton Railroad (KCR) information, ☎ 0-6069333.

Tram

The old imperial trams, covered with advertising, run between Kennedy Town and Shau Kei Wan on Hong Kong Island. They are inexpensive (HK60 cents) and easy to use since their route follows the harbour. Avoid using this means of transportation during rush hours.

Walking

Due to traffic congestion, walking in Hong Kong often involves dodging cars, buses and trams. Pedestrians are advised to be careful crossing streets and to keep in mind that people drive on the left. There remain, nonetheless, certain areas, particularly the parks, side-streets and markets, where walking can be a real pleasure. In one of its numerous brochures, the HKTA proposes several walking tours (Victoria Peak, the Botanical Garden and Bowen Road, B3-4 ; from Yau Ma Tei to Tsim Sha Tsui; the tomb of Li Cheng Uk and the resettlement zones; Western District and Cat Street, A2). You can easily explore the New Territories and the islands on foot.

HONG KONG IN THE PAST

Hong Kong's modern history begins with the arrival of the British, who began using the harbour in the 1820s to anchor their merchant vessels. Its history, though, predates the British presence and is an integral part of the history of China. Indeed, Hong Kong is a fragment of China, its population has always been predominantly Chinese, and—in the final analysis—when Hong Kong is returned to China in 1997, the British control of the territory will become a brief, though significant, interlude in the history of one of China's regions.

The story of this fragment of China is inextricably linked to the story of Western trade in the Far East and attempts to establish commercial ties with the vast empire of China, ties that were meant, above all, to be profitable to the West.

WESTERN TRADE WITH CHINA

The West began trading periodically with China in the early 16th century. When the Portuguese first acquired a base in Macau in 1557, the other European powers increased their efforts to establish trade relations with the Chinese kingdom. The Chinese authorities, however, were intent on keeping the foreigners, whom they regarded as barbarians, at bay. In 1715, the authorities opened Canton to Western traders but imposed severe restrictions on contact with the foreigners: they were given permission to reside during the trading season in the factory area of Canton; their families had to be left behind in Macau; commerce could be conducted only through the *Co-hong* merchants specially licensed to do business with the 'foreign devils' and who regularly (and arbitrarily, in the view of the Westerners) modified shipping dues with each transaction.

Enormous friction developed between the Chinese and the British, who dominated Western trade with Asia at the end of the 18th century. Their conceptions of everything from trade to justice to diplomatic relations differed radically. In particular, the Chinese expected all nations to accept their principles of judicial procedure and abide by the will of their emperor. The tension was to peak, and finally lead to war, over the traffic of opium.

OPIUM TRAFFIC

The British East India Company, which had a monopoly on British trade with China until 1834, grew opium in India and began selling the 'foreign mud'—as the Chinese called it—when they set up house in Canton in 1715. Throughout the 17th century, trade had been in China's favour with silver flowing into the country as the West bought silk, tea and other goods. The Westerners soon discovered that opium was the perfect product to counteract the West's trade deficit.

By 1799, opium was being imported in ever-growing quantities and the Chinese authorities, worried about the harmful effects of the drug and the flight of silver, officially banned the trade. The prohibition, though, only led to smuggling, with the British East India Company using intermediaries to avoid implicating the British government in the traffic. Chinese officials willing to defy the ban received substantial kickbacks. Opium traffic with China developed throughout the 19th century and more than doubled (from 20,000 to over 40,000 cases) in the period between 1833 and 1837.

In 1839, Emperor Tao Kuang dispatched the special commissioner Lin Tse-hsu to Canton to enforce the ban. He surrounded the factories and demanded that the foreigners surrender the opium. After a six-week siege, Captain Charles Elliot, the British Trade Superintendent, turned over more than 20,000 cases of opium (estimated value: two million pounds). Lin proceeded to burn all the opium stocks, half of which belonged to the British East India Company.

Outraged at Lin's action and unwilling to comply with his other demands concerning future trade relations, the British withdrew from Canton to Macau. There the Portuguese administration, eager to maintain good relations with the Chinese, refused to guarantee their safety. Practically the entire British community was evacuated to Hong Kong Island in merchant vessels that were anchored in its harbour. At the time, the mountainous island, with neither fresh water nor fertile soil, was inhabited by a small fishing population and frequented by pirates.

If Lin thought he had solved the conflict and put an end to the opium traffic, he was deeply mistaken. In London, the two Scottish founders of the British East India Company, William Jardine and James Matheson, were lobbying the British government to use military force against China. Their objective was to pressure the Chinese to allow unfettered trade. They also suggested that Hong Kong become a British outpost, thus allowing them to circumvent the Portuguese in Macau.

THE OPIUM WARS

In February 1840, Foreign Secretary Viscount Palmerston agreed to send an expeditionary force to Hong Kong in order 'to obtain reparations for insults, an indemnification for wrongful losses of merchants' property and security for future trade'. The war, known as the first Opium War, lasted until August 1842, when the Chinese, fearing further losses against the modern and better-

equipped British naval forces, signed the Treaty of Nanking. Besides opening five ports (Canton, Amoy, Foochow, Ningpo and Shanghai) to British traders, the Chinese ceded Hong Kong Island, put an end to the monopoly of the *Co-hong* and paid an indemnity equal to the British losses on the opium burned by Lin. Hong Kong was immediately declared a duty-free port.

Neither the British nor the Chinese were satisfied during the uneasy period of calm that followed. The Chinese authorities were powerless against the flow of opium, which continued as if trade had never ceased: 39,000 cases in 1845 and 52,000 in 1850 (when 20% of India's revenue came from its sale). The Chinese had lost face and, to a large extent, sovereignty over their own country. The British, on the other hand, had only partially accomplished their real purpose of opening China to unrestricted trade with the West. The Chinese continued to set duties arbitrarily and refused to give diplomatic status to Britain's representatives. What's more, Palmerston considered Hong Kong, which he described as 'a barren island with hardly a house upon it', to be a worthless acquisition.

In 1857, Chinese authorities boarded a vessel flying a British flag (but with an expired registration) and arrested some of the crew. The British used this minor incident as a pretext to attack Canton and head north towards Tientsin. They were supported by the French, who were seeking to avenge a French missionary executed for traveling in China without permission. The following year, the Treaties of Tientsin were· concluded, opening a further 11 ports to foreign trade, legalizing opium imports and allowing missionaries uninhibited travel within China. Yet, before the treaty could be ratified, British and French forces pushed on to the gates of Peking and secured further concessions, including the cession to the British of the tip of Kowloon Peninsula and Stonecutters Island in the Convention of Peking, signed in 1860.

These 'unequal' treaties, to use the Chinese expression, governed Chinese-Western relations until the end of World War II; the Chinese had lost the right to set customs tariffs and to enforce their own jurisprudence on foreigners. Foreign enclaves developed within China and, in the decades following the Convention of Peking, parts of the country were parcelled off to European countries and Japan. In 1898, the British requested and were given a 99-year lease on the New Territories (north of Kowloon to the Shenzhen River) and 235 outlying islands.

In the meantime, the opium traffic continued. The tide was not stemmed until the beginning of the 20th century, when China itself began producing opium. Its use was abolished in China in 1949, when the communists came to power. The British made it illegal in Hong Kong in 1946.

A BARREN ISLAND FLOURISHES

It is interesting to note that, during the crucial period that led to Britain's control of Hong Kong, the territory was never the central issue, neither in the Opium Wars nor in the resulting treaties. Palmerston's dismissive attitude towards Hong Kong was

Thousands of people live on junks and sampans in Aberdeen Harbour.

shared by politicians and merchants alike. Not even Jardine and Matheson were able to predict the rapidity of Hong Kong's growth. From the very outset, the colony flourished under the government's *laissez-faire* policies, becoming a major *entrepôt* and shipping centre. It also immediately became a magnet for Chinese immigrants seeking a place where their enterprising spirit could have free reign. The population of the colony swelled from 32,983 (31,463 Chinese) in 1851 to 878,947 (859,425 Chinese) in 1931.

Events in China continued to fashion the destiny of the British colony. Each crisis on the mainland had repercussions in Hong Kong. The overthrow of the Manchu dynasty during the Chinese revolution of 1911 sent thousands of Chinese across the border to the British colony. In the 1920s, in the aftermath of World War I, there was a rise of Chinese nationalism which spilled over the border. The Chinese were intent on eliminating the privileges of foreigners in their territories and putting an end to the unequal treaties. Foreign goods were boycotted and, in Hong Kong, a series of work stoppages developed into a prolonged general strike.

In 1938, the Japanese seized Canton, seven years after taking over Manchuria. In the shadow of the Japanese threat, 750,000 refugees sought shelter in Hong Kong between 1937 and 1939, bringing the population to 1.6 million on the eve of World War II. Three weeks after the attack on Pearl Harbour in December 1941, and 100 years after the founding of the colony, the Japanese invaded Hong Kong.

POST-WORLD WAR II DEVELOPMENTS

By the time the Japanese surrendered in August 1945, Hong Kong's economy was practically devastated, the territory was greatly in debt and poverty was everywhere. Many of its residents had fled to the neutral shores of the Portuguese colony of Macau or to mainland China. Yet Hong Kong quickly recovered. Trade doubled between 1946 and 1948 and its population once again grew from an estimated 600,000 at the end of the war to 1.8 million in 1947.

Since then, Hong Kong has experienced numerous waves of immigration that have become increasingly difficult to accommodate. The Chinese civil war (1948 to 1950) and the defeat of the nationalist government sent hundreds of thousands of 'White Chinese' across the border. Great Britain hastened to recognize the new communist government, which, isolated from most other countries, did not dare endanger the fabulous outlet for its trade that Hong Kong represented. Refugees from China (an estimated one million between 1949 and 1965) continued to flock to Hong Kong until the government took strict measures to stop immigration. By the mid-1970s, the Hong Kong government was sending illegal Chinese refugees back across the border.

Since the end of World War II, Hong Kong's economy has experienced almost constant growth, except for a brief stagnation in 1956 following the Korean War and the UN embargo on trade with China. Hong Kong's *entrepôt* trade suffered greatly but, once again, the colony demonstrated its capacity to adapt by diversifying into various manufacturing industries.

In 1967, in the aftermath of the Cultural Revolution in China, the communists of Hong Kong, encouraged by Canton's communist party, tried to turn a strike in a plastics factory into a general uprising. The police managed to maintain a British-style composure, while some bloody terrorist acts turned the general public against the communists. Peking, in the meantime, reprimanded the communist party in Canton which, it is thought, acted on its own initiative. Once again, China demonstrated that it was not about to snip off its money-making nose to spite its communist face.

1997: HONG KONG, CHINA

Yet, the status of Hong Kong remained unresolved: the British considered it a colony while the Chinese continued to regard Hong Kong as a Chinese territory administered by a foreign power. In December 1984, after 22 meetings, and not a few rumours and trial balloons, the diplomats produced the 'Sino-British Joint Declaration on the Future of Hong Kong'. It announced that on July 1, 1997 (the date when the British lease on the New Territories was to expire), all of Hong Kong would cease to be a British colony. Instead, under Deng Xiaoping's beloved 'one country, two systems' theory, it shall become the Special Autonomous Region of Hong Kong, China, with its own elected government, with freedom of speech, assembly, association, travel and religious belief. Moreover, it is to continue its capitalist way of life, and retain its own currency, for 50 years.

To draw up Hong Kong's constitution, known as the Basic Law, a 59-member committee was established including 25 Hong Kong representatives. A controversial draft of the constitution was made public by Peking in May 1988. The final version of the Basic Law will be drawn up by China in 1990, after consultation. Critics claim that neither the legal nor the electoral system will guarantee Hong Kong local control over its affairs and that the consultative bodies are to be dominated by pro-Peking representatives.

No one realistically expects a dramatic Indochinese-style exodus when July 1, 1997 arrives—no terrified families packed into leaky old boats in the South China Sea, waiting to be rescued. In fact, many Chinese will tell you they would prefer to stay. It is their home, after all. Those who can, however, are trying to obtain a foreign passport, as insurance just in case things go sour. Canada's are most desired (22,100 issued in 1987) since many of the applicants have relatives in Toronto and Vancouver; Australia (an estimated 10,000 visas in 1988) and the United States (with tougher restrictions—8,517 visas in 1987) are next. Everyone realizes that, theoretically, there is nothing that can stop Peking from tearing up the 'Sino-British Joint Declaration' if it wants to, and imposing its will directly on an autonomous Hong Kong, after July 1, 1997. No one, though, probably not even Peking, knows what lies in store for this once barren island and its 5.6 million inhabitants.

HONG KONG TODAY

S ituated on the south-east tip of China at about the same latitude as Calcutta and merely 74.6 mi/120 km from Canton, Hong Kong covers 413.5 sq mi/1071 sq km. It includes Hong Kong Island (known as 'the island' or 'Hong Kong side'), Kowloon Peninsula (across the harbour from Hong Kong Island), the New Territories (an area covering 355 sq mi/919 sq km north of Kowloon—stretching up to the 17 mi/27 km-long border with China's Guangchon province) and 235 mostly uninhabitable outlying islands in the surrounding waters.

Much of Hong Kong's vegetation has been destroyed over the past two centuries. Although projects of reforestation have been undertaken since World War II, only 13% of the land today is wooded. The territory has practically no natural resources. The absence of drinking water presents a serious problem. Every conceivable system has been tried to gather and store what precious rainwater falls in the region, but the colony remains almost totally dependent on mainland China for water.

A TINY ECONOMIC GIANT

How then, did a land devoid of natural resources and largely unsuited to urban development become one of the major commercial centres of the world? Hong Kong's two essential assets are its strategically located deep-water harbour and, above all, an enterprising and hard-working population. The British added the final touch: a free enterprise system with low taxes and high investment incentive. This recipe has produced spectacular commercial growth.

No territory the size of Hong Kong qualifies for as many superlative economic statements: it ranks as one of the world's busiest *entrepôt* ports; the world's leading container port (having surpassed New York and then Rotterdam in 1987); the third largest shipping centre after Japan and Greece; the third most important financial centre after New York and London; and the world's foremost toy exporter.

Shopping stalls line the busy streets of North Point.

Its economy is based on a delicate, but profitable, balance between imports and exports. Hong Kong imports almost all its food, water, raw materials, fuel and many of its consumer goods. It exports a variety of manufactured goods, including textiles, clothing, electronics, plastics, watches and more; the emphasis is on light manufacturing industrial production that can be housed in multi-storey factory buildings.

The textile and clothing industries account for about 42% of export revenues. The electronics industry is the second export earner (22%), followed by plastics (including toys), watches and clocks (each with a 10% share of export income). China and Japan are the two major countries of origin for imported goods, while the United States is the principal market for 'made in Hong Kong' merchandise.

Tourism, Hong Kong's third largest source of foreign exchange, is another key industry. More than 5.6 million tourists in 1988 brought in revenues of HK$33.3 billion, up 31% over 1987. More than one third of the tourists come from Japan and the United States.

Hong Kong is also one of the world's leading financial centres. In 1987, Hong Kong counted 154 full-service banks (many of them among the top banks in the world), 141 offices representing foreign banks, plus numerous deposit-taking institutions. Hong Kong's stock market, the largest in Asia outside Japan, attracts investors from around the world and provides a source of capital for local enterprises. Hong Kong also has an active commodity exchange, foreign exchange market and a gold and silver market.

Manufacturing industries employ 34.8% of the population and 43% of the manufacturing labour force is in the textile and clothing industry. The next most important sector is wholesale and retail trade, while restaurants and hotels account for another 23.2%. Unemployment is low, fluctuating from 1.8 to 3.8% between 1982 and 1987.

Labour legislation is minimal: only women and children benefit from regulations concerning work hours, supplementary hours and breaks. It is forbidden to employ children under 15, while women and young workers (aged 16 and 17) cannot work more than eight hours a day, six days a week. There is no minimum wage in Hong Kong but pay (an average of HK$121 a day in the manufacturing industries, for example) is decent by Asian standards. In the manufacturing sector, fringe benefits, such as free medical care and subsidized meals and transport, are common.

In 1987, there were 458 unions with only 368,090 members. The majority of the unions are affiliated with two large associations, each of which is aligned with foreign political powers. The Hong Kong and Kowloon Trades Union Council, with 69 affiliated unions mostly in the catering and building trades, is aligned with Taiwan, while the Hong Kong Federation of Trade Unions, with 78 affiliated unions mainly in shipyards, textiles, public utilities, printing and carpentry, is aligned with China. Strikes are becoming less frequent in Hong Kong, with most trade disputes arbitrated by the Labour Relations Board.

FROM BRITISH COLONY
TO CHINESE SOVEREIGNTY

Hong Kong's government is a typically colonial administration. Full powers are vested in the governor, who is appointed by the British monarch. He is advised on administrative questions by the Executive Council, which consists of four ex-officio members and 12 others appointed by the governor. The Legislative Assembly supervises territorial jurisdiction and public expenditure, while the Urban Council (for the metropolitan area) and the Regional Council (for the New Territories and the outlying islands) are in charge of public services (health, sanitation, etc.). In 1986, the first municipal elections for the Urban and Regional councils were held and, in 1985, 24 of the 56 members of the Legislative Assembly were for the first time selected in indirect elections. Direct elections for the Legislative Assembly, initially set for 1988, have been postponed until 1991, when only 10 members will be chosen directly by popular vote (16 indirectly and 30 appointed).

Despite these recent modifications (and unlike other British colonies that were encouraged after World War II to develop a democratic form of government), Hong Kong will go practically without transition from a colonial system of government to Chinese sovereignty. There are, of course, those who advocate wider democracy and franchise rights but the majority of Hong Kong residents are notoriously indifferent to political participation.

Of Hong Kong's 5,681,300 residents, 98% are of Chinese origin, mainly from the neighbouring province of Guangchon. Almost 60% of the population were born in Hong Kong. Cantonese is the native language for most Hong Kong residents, although English, the other official language, is used for administrative matters.

RELIGIOUS SYNCRETISM

Religious life in Hong Kong is characterized by a blend of Oriental philosophies and permeates every aspect of daily life. Elements from the teachings, beliefs and practices of Buddhism, Taoism and Confucianism are combined into a popular religion that heavily emphasizes ancestor worship. Except for the Buddhist monks or Taoist priests, few Chinese consider themselves to belong exclusively to one religion. They observe the moral precepts of Confucianism (not technically a religion); borrow from Buddhism its techniques of discipline and meditation and its theories concerning transmigration in the after-life; and believe in a host of Taoist deities and in Taoist practices of divination, magic and sorcery. Across the border, in mainland China, Confucianism reigns and the government actively discourages the superstitious practices of Taoism. Taoism, though, continues to flourish in Hong Kong as it does throughout the Chinese diaspora.

Each of Hong Kong's 360 Chinese temples is dedicated to one or two major deities, and often to several other minor ones. Other than Buddha, the major deities worshipped in Hong Kong are

Kwum Yum (the Buddhist goddess of mercy), Wong Tai Sin and Lui Cho (both Taoist gods) and, last but not least, Tin Hau (the goddess of heaven and protectress of seafarers). There are at least 24 temples honouring Tin Hau, with one in virtually every fishing village. During the Tin Hau Festival, tens of thousands of worshippers converge on the temple at Joss House Bay to celebrate the goddess's birthday (see p. 64).

Encouraged by Confucianist doctrines of filial piety and Buddhist concepts of after-life, ancestor worship is displayed in the elaborate rituals of burial, mourning and sacrifice. Every traditional Chinese home has a shrine dedicated to its ancestors four or five generations back. The family offers the dead all that they could have desired in life in the form of paper replicas of cars, houses, etc., which are burned at funerals, on the anniversaries of the birth or death and during festivals.

The cult of nature, another essential aspect of popular religion, is closely linked with the cult of ancestors. It is manifested in the widespread belief in the geomantic system of *fung shui* (literally, wind-water). *Fung shui* is based on the Taoist belief in the importance of the cosmic life force in determining man's place of dwelling and burial. The life force is composed of *yin*—the passive yielding principle—and *yang*—the active assertive principle—which interact and operate through the five agents: wood, fire, earth, metal and water. The *fung shui* expert is called on to indicate the propitious location, orientation and form of every building, road, grave or shrine to ensure prosperity and ward off evil forces.

Chinese medicine is fundamentally an attempt to re-establish the body's equilibrium of *yin* and *yang*. Acupuncture, the most important of traditional Chinese medicines and one which is increasingly used in the West, is based on the notion of achieving a balance between these forces within the human body. The Chinese also use an enormous variety of medicinal preparations to cope with everyday problems. Tired? A good soup of cobra blood will do the trick. Arthritic pains? Drink a tea prepared from tiger bones. The ashes of elephant skin are perfect to close up a wound. There are numerous, usually costly, remedies to stimulate virility. You can see all these potions and many more in the windows of Hong Kong's herbalists.

OVERPOPULATION AND HOUSING

Undoubtedly, Hong Kong's most significant social problem today stems from the rapid growth of its population, which has more than tripled since 1947. With 5,262 people per square kilometre, Hong Kong is one of the most densely populated countries in the world. Yet, as high as these figures are, they permit only a partial understanding of the enormity of the problem of overcrowding in the territory.

Three quarters of Hong Kong is covered with rugged hills unsuitable for use. A further 9% of the total area is devoted to agriculture and fish-farming. Thus, Hong Kong's population is concentrated into the remaining 16% of the territory. Approximately 3.5 million people reside in the areas around the harbour

The fishing industry, once an important economic activity in Hong Kong, still employs 24,000 people.

and 2 million in the eight New Towns (see p. 62) of the New Territories, bringing the density in the metropolitan sectors to 20,811 people per square kilometre. The remainder of the population is spread out in the small towns and hamlets dotting the New Territories and the outlying islands.

The government was at first reluctant to embark upon a construction program that would require significant capital expenditure. The first government housing project was built in 1955 after the disastrous fire at Shek Kip Mei, which left tens of thousands of people homeless. Today, the Hong Kong Housing Authority is the world's number one landlord, with almost half the population (some 2.7 million) residing in public housing. Both the public and private sectors have contributed to an incredible metamorphosis of Hong Kong over the past 30 years.

THE CHANGING FACE OF HONG KONG

The metropolitan areas have been completely transformed: massive housing developments have replaced the old dockyards; Ocean Centre and Harbour City (see p. 61) have gone up where the godowns (warehouses) used to be; on the Kowloon Peninsula the whole new sector of Tsim Sha Tsui East, complete with apartments, offices, hotels and shopping centres, has appeared where there was once only wasteland and sea, and in Central District on Hong Kong Island, new buildings are constantly altering the already impressive skyline. In the New Territories, villages have been swallowed up in the New Towns, with giant housing developments accommodating hundreds of thousands. Not even the size of the territory has remained constant: year after year it expands as land is reclaimed from the sea to make room for its ever-growing population.

Since 1972 the accent has been on the creation of New Towns built in the small market townships of the New Territories such as Sha Tin, Tai Po, Fanling, Yuen Long and Castle Peak. Each one accommodates between 100,000 and 700,000 inhabitants and has its own hospital, schools, police and fire departments, parks, open spaces and even cultural centres. More than half of all government expenditure since the beginning of the program has been spent on the construction of New Towns.

While these projects have contributed tremendously to easing overcrowding and have made Hong Kong a model of urban development, a shortage of decent housing continues to be a critical problem. What's more, conditions in the resettlement zones built in the 1950s leave much to be desired. Units of 376 sq ft/35 sq m often house seven or eight people who sleep in bunk beds. Up to 500 people use the only water source on each floor. Many of the early housing projects are already up for demolition and the government plans to replace them with more modern constructions.

In the private sector, the price of real estate is sky high. Rents for quality apartments and office space are among the most expensive in the world and keep rising as property owners attempt to make the most out of their investments before the 1997 deadline when the colony will return to Chinese sovereignty.

STEMMING THE TIDE OF IMMIGRATION

Meanwhile, 408,000 people are still living in precarious conditions in squatter villages or on sampans in the bay (though the government plans to rehouse them by 1992). The continual flow of legal and illegal immigrants from the Chinese mainland and the arrival of Vietnamese refugees are major obstacles in governmental attempts to reduce population *growth and provide sufficient housing. Each year almost 30,000 legal immigrants from China join their families in Hong Kong, while tens of thousands attempt to sneak across the border. In 1987, an average of 73 persons were arrested and repatriated each day and no one can accurately estimate the number of illegal immigrants who have escaped detection.

Since 1975, thousands of Vietnamese boat people have arrived annually on the shores of Hong Kong. There were approximately 10,000 Vietnamese refugees in refugee camps in 1987. At the beginning of 1988, the government decided to send back to Vietnam all those who could not prove that they left for political reasons: a condition that most would find difficult, if not impossible, to fulfill.

The key to Hong Kong's future lies in Peking. While there has never been an official Chinese diplomatic representation in Hong Kong, economic ties between the British colony and the mainland have always been strong.

THE CHINA-HONG KONG CONNECTION

Since 1985, Hong Kong has been China's principal commercial partner. In 1987, 31% of all Hong Kong's imports originated in

China, making it the number one supplier of goods. In turn, China is Hong Kong's second largest export market (accounting for 14% of total export revenues), behind the United States (with 37%). China supplies water to the colony and at least half of its food, while Hong Kong provides 40% of China's hard currency.

In 1985, China directly owned more than 300 companies (including 14 banks) in Hong Kong. In China, 75% of all joint ventures were established with investment capital from Hong Kong, while the Bank of China is the second largest bank in the colony with 50 subsidiaries.

More than one million Chinese work with Hong Kong companies in newly created Chinese sub-contracting and processing facilities, particularly in the Shenzhen special economic zone. Travel between the two countries is also on the rise, with 14.1 million Hong Kong residents crossing the border to the mainland in 1987, and 800,000 Chinese making the reverse trip to Hong Kong.

Hong Kong is of crucial importance to China's economy as an *entrepôt* centre, re-exporting Chinese goods to the West and vice versa. It also functions as China's bridgehead to the West, the ideal place to train its financial managers without having the corrupting influence of capitalists on the mainland.

AN UNCERTAIN FUTURE

As Hong Kong awaits its return to Chinese sovereignty, it is experiencing a flight of capital accompanied by a brain drain, especially among skilled workers and managers of banks and other financial institutions. Further dampening its economic outlook is the fact that its export economy is greatly dependent on global conditions: a recession in the major industrial nations would undoubtedly hit Hong Kong hard.

In the past, however, Hong Kong has shown a remarkable capacity to overcome economic setbacks. When its *entrepôt* trade slackened as a result of the UN embargo against China during the Korean War, Hong Kong diversified into light manufacturing and its economy was soon booming. Recently, the drop in the value of the US dollar and protectionist legislation in the United States (especially against textile imports) slowed the United States' consumption of Hong Kong merchandise. Hong Kong more than compensated for this loss of trade by selling more to countries where the lower dollar had increased their buying power (Hong Kong's dollar is pegged to the US dollar) and by increasing trade with China.

Finally, while certain investors and workers are fleeing, Hong Kong is becoming very attractive to those interested in investing in China. As a result, most economic analysts are predicting continued, though fluctuating, growth beyond 1997.

Hong Kong viewed from Victoria Peak. ➤

GETTING TO KNOW HONG KONG

Wandering around Hong Kong is a truly delightful experience. From skyscrapers to low-income housing projects, from temples and markets to beaches and 'floating towns', from duck-breeding farms and junk-building factories to barren islands and fishing villages: every nook and cranny is worth exploring. Your only problem will be to figure out where to start! The following section includes districts, sites, museums and gardens to visit in the four sectors of the territory: Hong Kong Island, Kowloon, the New Territories and the outlying islands.

HONG KONG ISLAND

Hong Kong Island covers approximately 29 sq mi/76 sq km. You can drive around the entire island in about an hour. We suggest starting your visit in the northern metropolitan areas along the harbour—Central District, Western District, Wan Chai and Causeway Bay. This is the core of Hong Kong, crammed with modern high-rise office buildings, residential sky-scrapers, shopping centres, hotels, restaurants and more. Don't miss the magnificent view from the 1,805 ft/554 m Victoria Peak, Hong Kong Island's highest point. Complete your tour of Hong Kong Island with a trip to the south coast: the fishing village of Aberdeen and the nearby aquatic centre of Ocean Park Water World, the beaches of Deep Water, Repulse and Big Wave bays and the markets of Stanley.

Central District **

Central District is the banking, financial and commercial hub of Hong Kong and many of the major hotels are located here. This is the capital of Hong Kong, officially known as Victoria, though no one uses that name. When the British first landed here, the harbour was about where Queen's Road Central (C3) is situated today: everything to the north has been built on land reclaimed from the sea.

Head south from the **Star Ferry Pier** (C2) towards **Statue Square** (C2). In this area are the major banks and business centres and many of the futuristic constructions that have gone up in the building spree which has taken place over the past decade. You will pass the **Jardine House** (C2; former Connaught Centre), with its round windows, where you can stop in at the main office of the **Hong Kong Tourist Association (HKTA)**. Among the recent development projects in the vicinity are: **Exchange Square,** Connaught Road Central (C2), right next to the Star Ferry, home to the stock exchange, where traders do their business sitting behind computer terminals; the **Far East Finance Centre,** Drake Street (C2), with its auspicious golden windows; **Bond Centre** and **Pacific Place,** both on Queensway Road (C3).

As befits one of the world's financial centres, two of Hong Kong's most interesting architectural achievements are its two largest banks. The **Hong**

Kong and Shanghai Bank, Queen's Road Central (C3), known simply as The Bank, hired the British architect, Norman Foster, to design a new headquarters. The 52-storey futuristic construction with exposed plumbing on the outside is reputed to be the most expensive office building in the world (officially, US$641 million). Not to be outdone, the communist-run Bank of China right next door, commissioned the Chinese-American architect, I.M. Pei, to design its new headquarters. At 70 storeys, it is Hong Kong's tallest building and cost merely an estimated US$141 million.

If you head west along Des Vœux Road, you will come upon a five-storey structure known as The Landmark (C2), which is built around a 20,000 ft/6080 m atrium containing hundreds of shops. Free entertainment is often given on a stage mounted above the fountain in the centre.

City Hall (CD2), to the east of the Star Ferry Pier, is the cultural centre of Central District. In the Low Block, there is a theatre and concert hall (open Mon-Fri 10am-6pm, Sat 10am-2pm; ☎ 5-739595). Entertainment information is available in the main lobby. The High Block houses the Hong Kong Museum of Art (open Mon-Wed, Fri and Sat 10am-6pm, Sun and holidays 1-6pm; ☎ 5-224127). The museum has a fabulous collection of Chinese antiquities and art from the 18th and 19th centuries.

Few colonial buildings have survived the successive waves of construction that continually sweep through Central District, particularly during the last 30 years. The oldest surviving colonial building in Hong Kong is the Flagstaff House Tea Wares Museum, off Cotton Tree Drive (C3; open Thurs-Tues 10am-5pm; ☎ 5-8690690). Built in 1844 as the official residence of the Commander of the British Forces, the museum has a fine collection of Chinese tea ware dating from the 3rd century until the present.

For a break from the hectic pace of Central District, visit the Zoological and Botanical Gardens, between Albert, Garden and Robinson roads (BC3-4; open daily 6am-7pm; admission free). It is small (12.5 acres/ 5.35 hectares), but has a fine collection of plants and animals. If you're an early riser, the best time to visit is between 6 and 8am, when it is filled with Hong Kong residents practicing *tai chi* before going to work. From Central District, you can either head towards Western District or up to the Peak.

Peak District **

Victoria Peak offers a breath-taking panorama of all Hong Kong. To get there from Central District, take the Peak Tram on Garden Road (C4) or bus n° 15 leaving from Exchange Square Bus Terminal (B2) right next to the Connaught Centre. If you prefer walking, follow the route recommended by the HKTA in its brochure entitled *A Fast Fact Guide* (available in HKTA offices, see pp. 11, 37).

The Peak is the most prestigious of Hong Kong's residential areas despite its extraordinary humidity and the fogs that frequently roll in and hide the view. You can stroll through its streets lined with terraced villas, walk around the lovely gardens that were part of the governor's residence (now demolished) at the turn of the century and dine at the Peak Tower coffee shop or restaurant.

Western District **

From Central District, you can walk to Western District (Sheung Wan) along Queen's Road Central or Des Vœux Road. It is quite a walk and you may prefer to hop onto a tram on Des Vœux Road or a bus marked Western Market. You can also take the MTR to Sheung Wan station.

This is one of Hong Kong's most picturesque areas. On either side of Hollywood Road (A2), west of Peel Street, are the famous 'ladder streets'—stone steps that climb from Queen's Road up to Caine Street. There are numerous small shops in this area filled with an incredible variety of merchandise. There are herbalists on Queen's Road West, snake shops on Jervois Street, merchants selling all kinds of eggs on Wing Sing Street, the renowned Cat Street Market and street stalls on Hollywood Road and Ladder Street. Shops will often stay open as late as 10pm and many remain open on Sunday.

Cat Street, also known as Upper Lascar Row, has all sorts of bric-a-brac for sale: used typewriters, pieces of jade, glasses, irons, dolls, musical instruments, furniture, odd shoes, earthenware, porcelain and more. It's a great place to go on a treasure hunt. Business has been sufficiently brisk for some antique dealers to set up shop on the more upmarket Hollywood Road.

Don't miss a visit to one of the oldest temples in Hong Kong—**Man Mo Temple****, at 124 Hollywood Road (A2). Built around 1847, this Taoist temple is dedicated to Kwan Kung, the god of war, and Mun Cheong, a civil god of literacy. Hanging from its roof are incense coils that are burned by worshipers in honour of these two gods and other subsidiary deities represented in the temple's panoply of polychrome images. Many Chinese come here to toss bamboo sticks and predict their future. The number of sticks that fall out of the container corresponds to a number on a series of boxes containing predictions for the future.

At night the Macau Ferry Wharf (A1) near the Hong Kong-China Ferry Terminal, turns into an open bazaar, known as the Poor Man's Nightclub (see p. 30).

Wan Chai, Causeway Bay and Happy Valley

Wan Chai was once famed for its nightlife (see p. 29). Today, it looks much like Central District, with its high-rise office buildings, hotels, restaurants and the new Hong Kong Convention International Exhibition Centre on Harbour Road. Two of Hong Kong's most important cultural institutions are located in Wan Chai. The **Hong Kong Arts Centre** (2 Harbour Rd., ☎ 5-280626) houses two theatres and a concert hall. Besides nightly performances, the renowned annual Arts Festival is held here in January. Across the street is the **Hong Kong Academy for the Performing Arts** (Harbour Rd., ☎ 5-8231500).

On Queen's Road East are numerous furniture stores and along the side streets are pet shops (selling snakes, birds, etc.). Further south on Bowen Road is **Lover's Rock** (Yan Yuen Shek). According to local legend, a beautiful woman who had lost her loved one came here, on the advice of a fortune-teller, and her prayers were answered. Women in search of good fortune in love come here on the 6th, 16th and 26th of each lunar month.

Continue east to Causeway Bay, once the site of the renowned company Jardine Matheson. Long overlooked by tourists, Causeway Bay has become one of the liveliest areas of the city, particularly for shopping, since the opening of the cross-harbour tunnel in 1972. The trendy Japanese department stores Sogo, Daimaru, Matsuzakaya and Mitsukoshi, popular among Hong Kong youth, are situated here. Many stores stay open until 9 or 10pm.

Causeway Bay is also a perfect place to eat supper, either in one of its great restaurants (see p. 28) or on a sampan that you can rent in the typhoon shelter opposite Victoria Park (see p. 37). The park is open around the clock and is a popular place for Hong Kong residents to practice *tai chi*, especially in the early morning. Nearby, opposite the Excelsior Hotel, is the legendary **Noonday Gun,** celebrated in the lyrics of Noël Coward's *Mad Dogs and Englishmen* ('In Hong Kong they strike a gong and fire off the Noonday Gun'). You can hear the gun each day at noon, of course, and at midnight on New Year's Eve.

Toward the southeast, off Tai Hang Road, are the **Tiger Balm Gardens**** (Aw Boon Haw Gardens; open daily 9am-4pm; admission free). Like its twin in Singapore, the gardens were made possible by a contribution from Mr. Haw (HK$16 million in 1935), the legendary inventor of the world-renowned miracle ointment, Tiger Balm. The gardens are unique, although

An incredible variety of merchandise is displayed in one of the Western District herbal shops.

the gaudy frescos and plaster statues of figures from Chinese mythology are not to everybody's taste. Mr. Haw's magnificent collection of jade is on display in **Haw Par Mansion** (☎ 5-616211). You can get to the gardens on bus n° 11 from Central Bus Terminal on Connaught Road. Further south is **Happy Valley Race Course,** one of Hong Kong's two racetracks (the other is at **Sha Tin,** see p. 36). As many as 50,000 fans gather here to watch and bet on the races every Wednesday evening and Saturday afternoon (and on some Sundays) from September to May.

Southern coast

Aberdeen is a good starting point for a tour of the south of Hong Kong Island. You can get there by bus n° 7 or n° 70 from Connaught Road Terminal (B2). This fishing village, among the oldest in Hong Kong, gives the visitor a brutal view of Hong Kong's changing society. There are an estimated 20,000 'water people' here, mostly of the Tanka and Hoklo ethnic groups. They are basically fisherfolk who live and work on their boats and their way of life has long been inextricably linked to the water. Today, there are still approximately 5400 people living crowded onto several hundred sampans and junks in the harbour. The government has relocated most of them in giant high-rise public housing. You can see one of these constructions, the massive and sinister Shek Pai Wan, towering over the disorder of sampans. In these buildings (scheduled to be replaced by more modern apartment buildings), conditions are only slightly better than on the junks and sampans. Moreover, for the water people, living on land poses some serious social and professional problems.

Many tourists come to Aberdeen simply to enjoy a meal on one of Aberdeen's floating restaurants (see p. 28). You can also explore the labyrinth of the floating town on a sampan or walk along the harbour and get a close look at the housing developments—one of the central aspects of modern life in Hong Kong (see 'Hong Kong Today', p. 50). As in other fishing villages, Aberdeen has a **temple** (built in 1851) dedicated to Tin Hau, the goddess of the sea. During the springtime Tin Hau Festival thousands of worshipers and hundreds of colourfully decorated boats converge on the Tin Hau Temple.

Situated between Aberdeen and Repulse Bay on Wong Chuk Hang Road is **Ocean Park ★★** (open Mon-Sat 10am-6pm, Sun and holidays 9am-6pm; ☎ 5-520291 or 5-556055). You can get to Ocean Park directly from Central District in about 30 minutes on the Ocean Park Citybus from Admiralty MTR station. This is a giant entertainment complex which includes a spectacular 29.6 ft/9 m deep Ocean Amphitheatre where dolphins and whales frolic; an artificial bay, Wave Cove, where seals, pelicans and penguins live in a reconstruction of their natural environment; a giant aquarium, Atoll Reef, which contains some 30,000 fish (including rays weighing 344 lbs/150 kgs); one of the largest roller coasters in the world; and several restaurants. Ride up in the cable car to the headland for a spectacular view of the South China Sea.

On weekends, especially in the summer, the city empties onto the four beaches on the southern and south-eastern coast of Hong Kong Island: **Repulse Bay** (200,000 people on Saturdays and Sundays), **Deep Water Bay, Shek O** and **Big Wave Bay.** They are less crowded on weekdays, but if you're looking for a secluded spot, you'd be better off trying the beaches of the New Territories (see p. 64) or of the outlying islands (see p. 66).

A few miles from Repulse Bay is **Stanley,** another one of Hong Kong's oldest villages. You can get here from Central District on bus n° 6 or n° 260 from Exchange Square Bus Terminal (B2), or from Causeway Bay on bus n° 63 on Tung Lo Wan Road. Stanley's chief attraction is its **flea market** (open daily 10am-7pm). Here, you can pick up designer clothes (or good imitations), American-style shirts, jeans, jackets and T-shirts at unbeatable prices. There are also boutiques selling basketware, porcelain, copper and 'made in China' products, all at bargain prices. The market is particularly busy on Sundays since it is one of the favourite shopping haunts of Hong Kong's residents.

▦ *KOWLOON PENINSULA*

On the other side of the harbour is Kowloon, a peninsula that covers only 3.75 sq mi/9.7 sq km. It stretches up to Boundary Street where the colony technically ends, although overcrowding in Kowloon has forced many buildings and factories over the border into the leased area of the New Territories. You can cross the harbour in no time by ferry, taxi (via the Cross Harbour Tunnel) or MTR.

Tourists spend more time in Kowloon than anywhere else in Hong Kong. Most of the hotels are situated here, and when visitors talk of a 'shopper's paradise', they are referring to Kowloon. On the southern tip of the peninsula are the lively and modern sectors of Tsim Sha Tsui and Tsim Sha Tsui East. Slightly to the north are the more traditionally Chinese districts of Yau Ma Tei and Mong Kok.

North of Boundary Street is an area that, although technically part of the New Territories, is administered and referred to as part of Kowloon. Places like Sham Shui Po, Lai Chi Kok, Lei Cheng Uk, the Kai Tak Airport and Wong Tai Sin are found on official maps of Kowloon and included in organized tours of the peninsula.

Just north of the airport is **Kowloon Walled City,** an area with no administrative status, belonging neither to Hong Kong nor to China (and left out of the Sino-British negotiations). The district, which the government intends to transform into a public park, is reputed to be frequented by thieves and outcasts and should be avoided by tourists.

Tsim Sha Tsui

The biggest hotels of Hong Kong and the largest shopping centres of Asia are located in this district. Start your tour of Tsim Sha Tsui in the shopping centres around the Star Ferry Pier (A3): **Ocean Terminal, Ocean Centre, Hong Kong Hotel** and **Star House.** Stop into **Harbour Village** (4th floor, Star House), where there is a wide selection of Chinese arts and crafts (woodwork, ivory carving, calligraphy, etc.). You can watch the craftsmen at work or have your fortune read here. To take a break from shopping, walk east on Salisbury Road (AB2) to the **Space Museum** (B2-3; open Wed-Mon 2-9:30pm; children under six not admitted; ☎ 3-7212361). There are daily shows at the **Space Theatre Planetarium.**

Further east on Salisbury Road is another huge shopping complex: the **New World Centre** (C2). Then comes the Tsim Sha Tsui East district, built in the 1980s entirely on land reclaimed from the sea. It is hard to imagine that a decade ago this area was deserted waterfront. Today, there are dozens of hotels (including the Regal Meridien, Kowloon, Shangri-La and Royal Garden) as well as shopping centres.

Backtrack to Nathan Road (B1-2), which divides Tsim Sha Tsui from north to south. Innumerable shops offering an extraordinary variety of merchandise line this road, known as the 'golden mile', and its side-streets. North on Nathan Road, at the entrance to the Kowloon Park (B1), is the **Kowloon Mosque** (B1), which was built in 1984 on the site of a mosque dating from the late 19th century (for a tour of the mosque, ☎ 3-7240095). You can also visit the **Hong Kong Museum of History** on Haiphong Road in Kowloon Park (B2; open Mon-Thurs and Sat 10am-6pm, Sun and holidays 1-6pm; ☎ 3-671124). In addition to changing historical and archaeological exhibits, the museum has an excellent collection of regional antiquities and old photographs of Hong Kong.

Yau Ma Tei *

Some of the atmosphere of old Hong Kong is preserved in the district of Yau Ma Tei between Jordan Road, Nathan Road, Man Ming Lane and the typhoon shelters. Take a bus along Nathan Road and get off near Jordan Road, or take the MTR to Jordan station. From here, you can meander along streets and alleys packed with a surprising array of shops. On Shanghai Street are *mah-jongg* shops and herbalists, and on Battery Street are wine merchants and stores selling paper replicas for funerals and ancestor-worship rites. There's a market on Reclamation Street, and lots more. For connoisseurs or curiosity-seekers, there is a fabulous **Jade Market** at the corner of Kansu and Reclamation streets (open daily 10am-3:30pm).

In the Yau Ma Tei typhoon shelter, the approximately 1000 sampans and junks (housing around 8000 persons) offer the same astonishing vista as Causeway Bay or Aberdeen.

Mong Kok *

Mong Kok is the most densely populated district in the territory. From Yau Ma Tei, continue north on Nathan Road or take the MTR to Mong Kok station. The Chinese come to this area to do their bargain hunting. On Tung Choi Street, just north of Soy Street, there's a **market** (open daily 1-11pm) for women's clothes and accessories. Sai Yuen Choi Street, one block to the west, is lined with shops selling hi-fi equipment. Mong Kok is less tourist-oriented than Tsim Sha Tsui and Yau Ma Tei, and English will not necessarily be spoken by local vendors, but the prices are significantly cheaper here. Don't miss the fabulous **Bird Market** * on Hong Lok Street, west of Nathan Road off Argyle Street. Here, you can see hundreds of varieties of birds, beautifully crafted bamboo cages and other accessories for bird-owners.

Northern Kowloon

Most of this area beyond Boundary Street is made up of large housing developments and industrial zones, but there are several places of interest to the tourist. You might want to have a look at the resettlement zones of Shek Kip Mei and Li Cheng Uk. They are examples of the poor living and sanitary conditions in the buildings constructed at the beginning of the government's housing program. Approximately 64,000 persons live in Shek Kip Mei housing, 48,000 in the Li Cheng Uk complex.

During the construction of Li Cheng Uk, the tomb of the Emperor Li Cheng Uk of the Han dynasty (AD 25-220) was unearthed. The archaeological finds are displayed in the burial vault, which has been transformed into a small **museum** (open Mon-Wed, Fri and Sat 10am-1pm, 2-6pm, Sun and holidays 1-6pm; ☎ 3-862863).

Farther along the north-western coast of the peninsula is the **Lai Chi Kok** district. Many tourists come here to spend an evening at the amusement park or to visit the **Sung Dynasty Village** ** at 11 Kau Wa Heng (open Mon-Fri for group visits through travel agencies, Sat and Sun for individual tours 12:30-5pm; ☎ 3-7415111). This is a sort of Disney World which re-creates a village from the Sung period (960-1179). There's a marketplace, a wine tavern and a tea house, plus villagers (fortune-teller, calligrapher, public writer, incense maker, etc.) dressed in period costume. Daily demonstrations include *kung fu*, acrobatics, traditional marriage ceremonies, performing monkeys and more. The village also houses a **Wax Museum** with effigies of 70 emperors and well-known figures of Chinese history.

On the north-eastern side of the peninsula, opposite the Wong Tai Sin Housing Development, is the **Wong Tai Sin Temple**. It is dedicated to a deified shepherd boy who learned how to transform cinnabar, a mineral used as a red pigment, into a substance conferring immortality. Believers come to this large and modern temple complex to be cured of illness or granted good fortune (particularly at the races). If you speak Cantonese, or are with someone who does, you can have your fortune told using bamboo sticks. While there is no admission charge to the temple, visitors are expected to leave a contribution.

▬▬ *NEW TERRITORIES*

Tourists rarely take full advantage of all the possibilities offered in the New Territories. It consists of numerous resettlement zones: 1.4 million of the

New Territories' two million inhabitants live in giant public housing projects, and upon completion of government development programs at the end of the 1990s, the population will have grown to 3.5 million. The New Territories, though, have much to offer the sightseer besides these often monstrous housing blocks: there are hundreds of small villages, tiny fishing centres, duck-breeding farms, shipyards, rice paddies where farmers still use water buffalo for ploughing, walled cities and beautiful countryside. If you travel through the New Territories on the main Kowloon-Canton railroad line (departing from the Hung Hom Station, see p. 39), we suggest that you stop off at Sha Tin, the Chinese University, Tai Po and Fanling/Sheung Shui. Otherwise the HKTA, and just about any tour operator organize tours of the New Territories. The following is a selective alphabetical listing of major towns and areas worth visiting in the New Territories and the places of interest in their surroundings.

Castle Peak

This was once the site of a village of the same name that, in 1973, became the industrial New Town of **Tuen Mun.** The countryside here is beautiful, wild and mountainous. It's a great place for walking. There are several pleasant beaches along the coast of Castle Peak Bay.

Nearby, amid beautifully landscaped greenery, is the **Ching Chung Koon Temple**.** It was built recently (1959), but contains many ancient treasures including a 1000-year-old jade seal. The temple's lanterns are more than two centuries old and come from the Imperial Palace. The temple is dedicated to Lui Tung Bun, one of the eight Taoist immortals, responsible for eliminating evil from the world. On the grounds, there is a home for the elderly. Visitors can eat in the temple's vegetarian restaurant. Further north is the **Miu Fat Monastery** and its ornate, three-storey Buddhist temple. Two dragons, 20 ft/6 m high, guard the entrance.

Take the MTR to Tseun Wan station and then bus n° 68 or n° 68M to Castle Peak and the Miu Fat Monastery, or bus n° 66M to Ching Chung Koon Temple.

Fanling and Sheung Shui

Sheung Shui is the last stop on the Kowloon-Canton line for those without a Chinese visa. A small market with water-buffalo tanneries is worth visiting in Sheung Shui. A New Town encompassing Fanling and Sheung Shui plus the neighbouring villages of Luen Wo Hui and Shek Wu Hui is under construction. The current population of 110,000 is expected to double by the end of the 1990s. There are several golf courses at Fanling's **Royal Hong Kong Golf Club** (open to visitors by appointment and on a first-come, first-served basis Mon-Fri; ☎ 0-901211). Nearby is the **Luen Wo Market.** The best way to get to Sheung Shui is via the Kowloon-Canton railway line.

Kam Tin Walled Villages**

Not far from Yuen Long, you can visit six walled villages that were built in the 17th century. The walls afforded the inhabitants protection against pirates and bandits. **Kat Hing Wai** and **Shui Tau** are the best preserved among them. They have become popular tourist destinations, especially Kat Hing Wai. Villagers wear period costumes (the women's hats are brimmed with black cloth fringes). The streets are lined with souvenir stands. You should ask permission before photographing the villagers and expect to pay. In Shui Tau, there is a **Tin Hau Temple** built in the early 18th century.

Take the MTR to Tsuen Wan station and then bus n° 51 at the Tsuen Wan Bus Terminal (a short walk away) directly to the villages.

Lau Fau Shan and Yuen Long

Jutting out into Deep Bay on the north-west tip of the New Territories is Lau Fau Shan. This is a huge fish market surrounded by duck and fish farms and oyster beds. There are dozens of indoor and outdoor restaurants and you can select a fish from the marketplace and take it to a restaurant to be prepared. Lau Fau Shan used to be renowned for its oysters but pollution in Deep Bay has ruined what was once a thriving local trade and the edible oysters are now imported from China (avoid eating raw oysters).

Nearby, you can stop at another of the territory's New Towns, Yuen Long, which used to be a small market town and now has a population of 110,000.

Take bus n° 68X from Jordan Road Bus Terminal in Kowloon to Yuen Long; Light Rail Tourist Feeder bus n° 655 to Lau Fau Shan.

Plover Cove Reservoir

Plover Cove was made into a reservoir in 1968 in an attempt to supply Hong Kong with much-needed fresh water. The surrounding countryside is great for hiking. There are streams and a lovely waterfall (which flows into the reservoir) at **Bride's Pool**. The area got its name from a local legend: a bride on her way to her wedding in a nearby village fell from the sedan chair when one of the bearers slipped and plunged down the waterfall to her death. There are numerous nature trails in this beautiful wooded area. Pick up information and maps at the **Tai Mei Tuk Visitors Centre** (open Wed-Mon 9:30am-noon, 12:30-4:30pm; ☎ 0-6563413).

From the Tai Po Market Kowloon-Canton railway station, take the Kowloon Motor Bus (KMB) n° 75R on Sundays and holidays to the start of the Bride's Pool Nature Trail; the KMB n° 75K from Monday to Saturday to Tai Mei Tuk.

Sai Kung Peninsula**

Here, you will find some of the most beautiful countryside in the territory and several of Hong Kong's most secluded beaches. Almost all of the interior of the peninsula is 'protected country park' without any motorized traffic and with extensive hiking trails. **Hong Kong Government Publications** (GPO Bldg., Central District, Hong Kong Island) publishes numerous brochures on trails and detailed maps.

Some of Hong Kong's most beautiful secluded beaches are located on the Sai Kung Peninsula, particularly along the coast of **Hebe Haven, Tolo** and **Mirs Bays.**

After seeing so many crowded housing blocks in the New Territories, you might want to have a look at how some of Hong Kong's rich residents live. Head south on the Sai Kung Peninsula past luxury villas to the resort area of **Clearwater Bay.** Overlooking beautiful beaches is the exclusive **Clearwater Bay Golf and Country Club.** Besides golf courses, there are saunas, a jacuzzi, a swimming pool, tennis and squash courts, and more. Contact the HKTA for more information (see p. 37). Note that the beaches of the bay are extremely crowded on summer weekends.

Farther south at Joss House Bay is the biggest **Tin Hau Temple*** (also known as Da Miao) in Hong Kong. Built in the 13th century, this is a site of lavish festivities during the celebration of the birthday of Tin Hau in the spring (see p. 24).

Take bus n° 5 from Star Ferry Terminal to Choi Hung Bus Terminal and then bus n° 92 to the town of Sai Kung or n° 91 to Clearwater Bay.

Sha Tin Valley*

Sha Tin, once a small township, is now a modern metropolis with a population of about 460,000 and plans to accommodate another 300,000 by the mid-1990s. In the centre of Sha Tin New Town, you'll find the **Sha Tin Cultural Complex, New Town Plaza** (a gigantic shopping centre) and **Sha Tin Central Park.**

A 30-minute walk from the Sha Tin train station, on a hill overlooking the valley, is the **Temple of Ten Thousand Buddhas**, one of the most renowned temples in Hong Kong. According to the HKTA, there are 12,800 Buddhas, each slightly different, on the temple's walls. The complex consists of several pavilions and a bright red pagoda.

On another hill overlooking Sha Tin is **Amah Rock,** a local monument and place of worship. According to legend, a fisherman's wife came here daily with her baby on her back waiting for her husband to return, obstinately refusing to believe that he was dead. The gods took pity on her and sent forth a lightning bolt, which carried them to heaven to join the fisherman and left the rock in their place.

Also in Sha Tin is Hong Kong's second **racetrack,** which was inaugurated in 1978. It was entirely constructed on reclaimed land, has computer-operated betting, air-conditioned stables and is said to have been the most costly racetrack in the world. Like at Happy Valley, races are held on Wednesday nights and Saturday afternoons (and some Sundays) from September to May.

Immediately north of Sha Tin (along the railway route to Tai Po) is the **Chinese University,** built in 1963. The Institute of Chinese Studies has an **art gallery** (open Mon-Sat 9:30am-4:30pm, Sun and holidays 12:30-4:30pm; ☎ 0-6952218 ext. 218) with an extensive collection of antique bronze seals and Chinese paintings and calligraphy. From here you can take a sampan to the Sai Kung Peninsula.

You might also visit the 19th-century **Tsang Tai Uk Walled Village** nearby. It is not as ancient as Kam Tin but neither is it as commercial.

Take the Kowloon-Canton railway line to Sha Tin or Ma Liu Shui (for the university).

Tai Po *

Tai Po was once a small market town where people from surrounding areas came to buy and sell produce, fish and merchandise. All this has changed with the construction of housing accommodating 150,000 people (and expected to house 290,000 by the mid-1990s). Yet Tai Po retains a touch of its lively and rural ambience. Some fishermen still live in huts built on pile foundations. Worth visiting is the **Tai Po Market,** with its fish and vegetable stalls. At the **Tai Pin Carpet Factory ★★** on Ting Kok Road (☎ 0-6565161 ext. 211), you can buy exceptional carpets or simply watch demonstrations of the art of Chinese carpet-making. The best way to get here is via the Kowloon-Canton railway line.

Tsuen Wan

The last stop on the MTR line, just beyond northern Kowloon, is the New Town of Tsuen Wan. Approximately 700,000 people live in its housing blocks and work in its industrial zone or in the Kwai Chung container port (the world's busiest). The factories and housing were constructed on land reclaimed from the sea, as was the container port. A popular local pastime is to prepare a picnic, rent a sampan or junk at the port and spend the day fishing and playing *mah-jongg.*

Take the MTR to Tsuen Wan station.

▬ *OUTLYING ISLANDS*

Just before your plane lands in Hong Kong, you can catch a glimpse of the magnificent mountainous scenery of Hong Kong's 235 islands. Many are less than one hour by ferry from Hong Kong Island and present a fabulously surrealistic contrast to the frenzy of the city. Like the junks in the bay, the islands belong to the past. Yet while the wine-coloured sails have gradually disappeared, the islands remain a living monument to days gone by. Here, the islanders still observe traditions long forgotten elsewhere.

There are regular ferries from Central District to the islands of Lantau, Lamma, Cheung Chau and Peng Chau. For departure information, call the **Hong Kong and Yau Ma Tei Ferry Company** (☎ 5-423081). Be aware that these islands, and the ferries, tend to be particularly crowded on summer weekends. Lantau is the only outlying island where there are roads built for cars. To get to the other islands, you will have to rent a sampan or junk either at the harbour or directly from one of the four major island piers. For information on junk rentals, call the Boating Centre, ☎ 5-223527.

The HKTA puts out a free brochure entitled *Outlying Islands*. It will guide you through the outlying islands, their beaches, towns, monasteries, etc. Serious hikers can purchase detailed maps of the islands from **Hong Kong Government Publications** (GPO Bldg., Central District). The HKTA can also supply you with a complete listing of accommodation on the islands. Renting rooms is possible on the more inhabited islands, but to find them and negotiate the price, you'll need to speak Cantonese (or find someone who does).

Cheung Chau**

Cheung Chau used to be an infamous pirate haunt and numerous pirate caves can still be found here to prove it. Today, this is Hong Kong's most densely populated outlying island. There is a town built around the harbour with numerous shops and restaurants lining the side-streets.

Many of the island's inhabitants live on junks and sampans in the sea, and fishing is still the island's main industry. On the waterfront in the north, there are also junk-building factories where traditional boat construction continues almost as it did a century ago. Cottage industries include the manufacture of shrimp butter, biscuits and playing cards. You can dine in one of the island's great seafood restaurants: the beachside **Cheung Chau Country Club,** in particular, is a pleasant place to have a meal. The **Pak Tai Temple,** built in 1783, is the centre of the Bun Festival celebrations in May (see p. 24).

There are 34 ferries leaving daily from Outlying Districts Ferry Pier, Central District (B1), between 6:25am-1:30pm. The last ferry returns to Hong Kong Island at 10:30pm. The trip takes one hour.

Lamma*

Lamma is a great place for a leisurely walk or swim. It is sparsely populated, with numerous trails for exploring and lovely beaches for relaxation. There are also good restaurants in the villages of **Sok Kwu Wan** and **Yung Shue Wan.** Stalls lining the narrow streets of Yung Shue Wan sell shrimp paste, dried fish, Chinese herbs and more.

Ferries for Sok Kwu Wan and Yung Shue Wan leave from Central Harbour Services Pier (B1), Mon-Fri 8am-10:30pm, Sat and Sun 7:30am-10:45pm. The trip takes 40 minutes.

Lantau**

Lantau is the largest of Hong Kong's outlying islands, almost twice the size of Hong Kong Island, but with a population of less than 16,000. The main economic activities are fishing and fishing-related industries, duck-breeding and rice cultivation. Almost half of the island's population lives in the fishing port and market town of **Tai O.** In any of Tai O's lovely seafood restaurants, you can sample locally made shrimp paste.

The most popular tourist destination on Lantau is the richly decorated Buddhist **Po Lin Monastery*.** To get there, take a direct bus to the monastery from Silvermine Bay. A statue of Buddha (112 ft/34 m, the tallest in South-East Asia) is being constructed just outside the monastery. For a nominal cost, you can eat a delicious vegetarian meal served in the monastery's dining room. You can also stay overnight in the rural dormitory (an unforgettable experience). If you're up to it, climb the hill overlooking the monastery at sunrise: it's a perfect place to meditate.

Lantau also has a **Trappist monastery** that is more isolated than the Po Lin Monastery. It is accessible by boat from Peng Chau. The monks have taken a vow of silence and visitors are expected to observe the silence too. If you would like to visit or stay overnight at the monastery, write in advance to the Grand Master, Trappist Haven, Lantau Island, PO Box 5, Peng Chau, Hong Kong.

The island's most beautiful beach is **Cheung Sha,** which is along the Silvermine Bay/Po Lin bus route. Other places worth visiting are the magnificent **Shek Pik Reservoir,** surrounded by lovely footpaths, and the **Tung**

The colourful Pak Tai Temple on Cheung Chau Island.

Chung Fort, an imperial outpost built in the late 18th century.

Ferries for Silvermine Bay (Mui Wo) leave from the Outlying Districts Ferry Pier, Central District (B1). There are 18 daily ferries during the week, and 20 on weekends, 7am-11:15pm. The last ferry returning to Hong Kong Island leaves at 10pm. The trip takes one hour and 15 minutes.

Peng Chau

There are 10,000 inhabitants on Peng Chau, the smallest of Hong Kong's four major islands. In addition to fishing, cottage industries such as the creation of hand-painted porcelain **(Hop Woo Lung Chinaware Factory)**, woodwork and wickerwork are practiced. Near the harbour, you can buy seafood directly from fishermen and have it prepared at one of the nearby restaurants. From Peng Chau, you can take a sampan to the Trappist monastery of Lantau.

From Outlying Districts Ferry Pier, Central District (B1), there are 18 daily ferries, 7am-11:15pm. The last ferry returning to Hong Kong Island leaves at 10:10pm. The trip takes one hour.

Po Toi

The deserted houses and strange rock formations on this island, situated in the south of the territory, endow it with an air of mystery. There are several restaurants near the ferry pier.

From Stanley, there are weekend departures at 10 and 11:30am, returning ferries at 3, 4:30 and 6pm.

INTRODUCTION TO MACAU

The Portuguese-administered territory of Macau, a peninsula on the south coast of China, is only a one-hour boat ride from Hong Kong. A great place for leisurely sightseeing, this duty-free port is known more as a gambling centre, the 'Las Vegas of the East', than as a tourist destination in its own right. Most of Macau's more than five million annual tourists—more than 80% Hong Kong Chinese—come here because gambling is legal. Macau casinos, open around the clock, offer all the usual Western games (black-jack, baccarat, roulette, etc.), plus Chinese games such as *fan tan* and *dai-sui*. Other attractions include jai alai matches, greyhound and horse racing as well as the annual Macau Grand Prix in November.

Yet, Macau has much to satisfy the curious tourist beyond its casinos, discos and nightclubs. Tourists will find it a welcome change from the hustle and bustle of the British colony. Here, the pace is more relaxed and, unlike Hong Kong, Macau's historical sites have not been uprooted to make room for modern skyscrapers and housing developments. Ceded to the Portuguese in 1557, this is the oldest remaining European colony in Asia. Here, history lives on, ever present along the winding cobble-stoned streets of the city. You can visit numerous well-preserved Buddhist or Taoist temples, Catholic churches ornamented with Christian motifs in an Oriental style, typically Portuguese manors and palaces, as well as rural villages and farming settlements on the islands of Taipa and Coloane.

The intermingling of Portuguese and Chinese cultures endows Macau with an unusual and unique charm: Asian faces framed in the windows of Portuguese-style houses, pedicabs and sampans, streets named after Catholic saints and Portuguese heros tran-scribed in Chinese letters. The festival calendar includes Chinese, Christian and Portuguese holidays. The food is an exotic and delicious blend of Portuguese and Chinese ingredients with those from the former Portuguese colonies of Africa. Macau today is a paradoxical product of the Christian West and the Far East. It is most definitely worth a detour.

Macau in brief

Location: Macau extends from the south coast of China, 37.5 mi/60 km west of Hong Kong.

Area: 6.17 sq mi/16 sq km, including the islands of Taipa and Coloane.

Population: 433,000 inhabitants, of which 95% are Chinese.

Capital: Macau.

Religion: Catholicism is the official religion. Buddhism, Taoism and Confucianism are widely practiced.

Language: Portuguese is the official language, although the Cantonese dialect of Chinese is more widely spoken. English is spoken in the majority of tourist sites.

Political status: Macau has been a Portuguese-administered territory since 1557. According to the 1987 agreement (see p. 83), Macau will be returned to China December 20, 1999 while preserving a special status.

Economic activity: Manufacturing of textiles and tourist-related service industries.

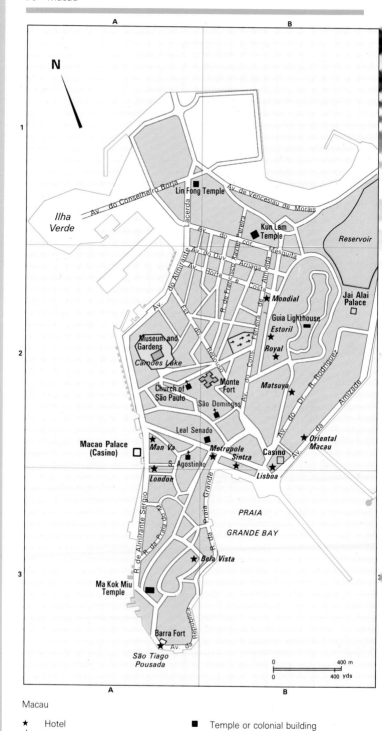

Macau

★ Hotel
✚ Church

■ Temple or colonial building
□ Casino

PLANNING YOUR TRIP

WHEN TO GO

Situated in the tropics, Macau is generally hot and humid with temperatures averaging 68° F/20° C. The best time to visit is during the dry months of October and November when it is sunny and temperatures are mild. January and February tend to be cool but sunny, with temperatures around 57° F/14.6° C. During the monsoon season, from April to September, there are frequent downpours and the humidity is high. The summer months are hot, rainy and humid and can be extremely unpleasant, especially in July when temperatures average 82° F/28.3° C (for average temperatures, see Hong Kong section, p. 9).

GETTING THERE

It is easy to get to Macau via Hong Kong (for information on getting to Hong Kong, see p. 9). The trip takes 55 minutes by jetfoil, 75 minutes by hydrofoil, 90 minutes by the high-speed ferry and at least three hours by the regular ferry. Try to avoid travelling during weekends when boats tend to be overcrowded. All departures are from the Macau Ferry Terminal, 200 Connaught Rd., Hong Kong Island (A1).

Jetfoil

There are 45 departures daily from 7-2:30am. A one-way economy ticket for this 55-minute trip costs HK$57 from Monday to Friday, HK$63 on weekends and HK$77 after 6:30pm. For information, call **Far East Jetfoil Company** (☎ 5-8593111). For telephone reservations with credit card, ☎ 5-8593288. Tickets can be picked up in advance at 'Ticketmate' windows at the MTR stations of Tsim Sha Tsui, Jordan, Mong Kok, Causeway Bay, Wan Chai, Tsuen Wan and Kwun Tong.

Hydrofoil

There are departures approximately every 20 minutes from 8am-6pm. The ticket for this 75-minute trip costs HK$58 from Monday to Friday, HK$46 on weekends. For information, call **Hong Kong and Macau Hydrofoil** (☎ 5-218302).

High-speed ferry

There are five daily departures from Monday to Friday, and six on weekends, from 8am-8pm. The ticket for this 90-minute trip costs HK$46 in first class and HK$38 in second class.

Ferry

There are departures from Monday to Thursday at midnight, on Friday at 2:30pm, on Saturday at 10am and 2:30pm and on Sunday at 9:30pm. The one-way ticket costs HK$30. When the weather is nice, the trip along the South China coast is extremely enjoyable. Certain ferries are equipped with television lounges, a bar, passenger cabins and slot machines (that can be used only in the territorial waters of Macau). The trip takes about three hours.

ENTRY FORMALITIES

Passport and visa

Don't forget your passport. Citizens of Australia, Canada, Great Britain and the United States do not require a visa if they plan to stay less than 90 days. However, if you do need a visa, you can get one on arrival in Macau. They cost M$52 and are valid for 20 days. You can also get a visa from the Portuguese Consulate in Hong Kong (room 1405, Central Bldg., 3 Pedder St., Central District, ☎ 5-231338).

Vaccinations

No vaccinations are required unless you are coming from a cholera-infected area.

Customs

You can bring almost anything into Macau (except prohibited drugs and firearms) and there are no export duties on anything bought in Macau. However, remember that Hong Kong customs will only allow one quart bottle of alcohol and 50 cigarettes to enter duty-free and your bags will almost certainly be checked when you return from Macau.

MONEY

The unit of currency is the *pataca* (M$), divided into 100 *avos*. It is worth slightly less than the Hong Kong dollar but, in Macau, the two currencies are interchangeable. (This is not true in Hong Kong, where the exchange rate is not good.)

Notes are in denominations of M$5, M$10, M$50, M$100 and M$500. Coins are 10 *avos*, 20 *avos* and 50 *avos*, M$1 and M$5.

Travellers' checks and most credit cards are accepted everywhere. Often, however, you will pay less if you use cash.

WHAT TO TAKE (see Hong Kong section, p. 11).

BEFORE YOU LEAVE: SOME USEFUL ADDRESSES

The **Macau Tourist Information Bureau** has many overseas offices, including the following:

Australia

Suite 604, 135 Macquarie St., Sydney, NSW 2000, ☎ (02) 241 3334, toll free (008) 252 448.

Canada

Suite 304, 1385 West 8th Ave., Vancouver B.C. V6H 3V9, ☎ (604) 736 1095.

Suite 308, 150 Dundas St. West, Toronto ONT M5G 1C6, ☎ (416) 593 1811.

Great Britain

Airwork House, 35 Piccadilly, London WN 9PB, ☎ (01) 734 7282.

United States

Suite 309, 608 Fifth Ave., New York, NY 10020, ☎ (212) 581 7465.

3133 Lake Hollywood Dr., PO Box 1860, Los Angeles, CA 90078, ☎ (213) 851 3402, toll free in California: (800) 331 7150.

PRACTICAL INFORMATION

ACCOMMODATION

Macau has several luxury hotels. Fine accommodation is also available in many of the old-fashioned and charming inns and villas of Macau. Reservations (highly recommended for weekends and on special occasions) can be made through any Hong Kong travel agency and the **Macau Tourist Information Bureau.** You can obtain a complete listing of hotels from the tourist office (see pp. 72, 80). For an explanation of hotel categories, see Hong Kong section, p. 13.

Map coordinates refer to the map p. 70.

▲▲▲▲ **Hyatt Regency,** Taipa Island, ☎ 27000 (or 5-590168 in Hong Kong, telex: 88512 HY MAC OM). Located across the bridge from the city, this hotel offers a choice of restaurants, a swimming pool, a casino and a disco. 356 rooms.

▲▲▲▲ **Mandarin Oriental Macao,** Avenida da Amizade (B3), ☎ 567888 (or 5-487676 in Hong Kong), telex: 88588 OMA OM. This hotel is the Macanese sister to the luxurious **Mandarin Oriental** of Hong Kong. Close to the ferry terminal, with casino, health club, tennis courts, European and Chinese cuisines. 438 rooms.

▲▲▲▲ **Pousada de São Tiago,** Avenida da República (A3), ☎ 78111 (or 5-8108332 in Hong Kong). Classic, exclusive inn built within the walls of a 17th-century fortress. Cross-harbour view of mainland China, swimming pool, Portuguese and French cuisines. 23 rooms.

▲▲▲ **Lisboa,** Avenida da Amizade (B3), ☎ 377666 (or 5-591028 in Hong Kong), telex: 88203 HOTEL OM. The Lisboa's 'sputnik' design makes it an unmistakable, if tacky, landmark. Five restaurants, boutiques, pool, floor show and Macau's top casino. 750 rooms.

▲▲▲ **Presidente,** Avenida da Amizade (B2), ☎ 553888 (or 5-266873 in Hong Kong), telex: 88440 HPM OM. This hotel offers a choice of European, Chinese and Korean cuisines, and has a trendy nightclub. 340 rooms.

▲▲▲ **Royal,** Estrada da Vitoria (B2), ☎ 552222 (or 5-422033 in Hong Kong). This hotel is well-equipped, with health club, gym, squash court, indoor pool, disco and European, Japanese and Chinese restaurants. 380 rooms.

▲▲ **Estoril,** Avenida Sidonio País (B2), ☎ 572081/3 (or 5-221832 in Hong Kong). Located in a residential district, this hotel has a swimming pool, a sauna and a Chinese restaurant. 89 rooms.

▲▲ **Metropole,** 63 Rua da Praia Grande (B2), ☎ 88166 (or 5-406333 in Hong Kong), telex: 88356 CTSMACAO OM. This hotel houses a travel agency and a European restaurant. 110 rooms.

▲▲ **Pousada de Coloane,** Praia de Cheoc Van, Coloane Island, ☎ 328143/328144 (or 3-696922 in Hong Kong). Modern inn overlooking beach, with large terrace and swimming pool. 22 rooms.

▲▲ **Sintra,** Avenida Dom João IV (B2), ☎ 85111 (or 5-408028 in Hong Kong), telex: 88324 SINTRA OM. This hotel has a sauna, a 24-hour coffee shop and a restaurant serving Chinese and European cuisines. 236 rooms.

▲ **Bela Vista,** 8 Rua Comendador Kou Ho Neng (A3), ☎ 573821. Although modest, this colonial-style hotel has a lot of character and is a favourite with foreigners working in Hong Kong. Veranda restaurant overlooking Macau-Taipa bridge. 23 rooms.

▲ **Central,** 26 Avenida Aleida Ribiero (A2), ☎ 77700. The rooms here are clean and air-conditioned. 160 rooms.

▲ **London Hotel,** Ponte E. Horta (A2), ☎ 83388. This is a nice, clean hotel with small, but comfortable, rooms.

▬▬ BUSINESS HOURS

Most offices are open Monday to Friday 9am-1pm, 3-5:30pm, Saturday 9am-1pm. Banks are open Monday to Friday 10am-1pm, 3-4pm. Casinos are open 24 hours, seven days a week. Shops are open every day of the year except for several days around Chinese New Year. They generally remain open to 5 or 6pm.

▬▬ CONSULATES

All foreign consulates to Macau are located in Hong Kong (see p. 23).

▬▬ CURRENCY EXCHANGE

You can change foreign currency or travellers' checks in banks. There are also money-changers in the big hotels and in the casinos (where they are open 24 hours). Since Hong Kong dollars are freely negotiable in Macau while *patacas* are difficult to change, even in Hong Kong, it is best to exchange as little money as possible and use up all your *patacas* before leaving to avoid costly reconversion. Be aware, however, that buses in Macau will not accept Hong Kong money, so if you intend to take a bus from the ferry, be sure to get some *patacas* before leaving Hong Kong.

▬▬ ELECTRICITY

In most hotels, on the islands and in the more modern areas of Macau, the electricity is 220 volts. In some districts on the peninsula the power supplied is 110 volts.

▬▬ EMERGENCIES

Ambulance: 3300.
Fire department: 572222.
Police: 999.

▬▬ FESTIVALS AND PUBLIC HOLIDAYS

Macau, like Hong Kong, celebrates all the Chinese festivals, as well as Catholic, and some specifically Portuguese, holidays. The Chinese New Year and other Chinese festivities are inevitably accompanied by electrifying fireworks displays; they can be even more sensational than in Hong Kong, where fireworks are banned (for a description of the major Chinese festivals, see the Hong Kong section, p. 24). The **Macau Tourist Information Bureau** (see pp. 72, 80) can supply you with a program of annual holidays and festivals and their exact dates. The following is a list of the major Catholic holidays and Portuguese anniversaries celebrated in Macau:

February and March

Procession of Our Lord of Passos: Specifically Macanese, this is one of the city's most jubilant Catholic holidays. On the first Saturday evening of Lent, the statue of Jesus is taken from the altar of St Augustine's Church and carried to the cathedral, where an all-night vigil takes place. The following day, after high mass, a procession accompanies the statue through the stations of the cross set up in the streets of the city and back to the altar of St Augustine's.

April and May

Anniversary of the 1974 Portuguese Revolution (April 25): This is a public holiday commemorating the left-wing coup d'état.

Labour Day (May 1): This is a public holiday.

Feast of Our Lady of Fatima (May 13): On this day, Catholics commemorate the miracle of the apparition of the Virgin to three young shepherds in Fatima, Portugal, in 1917. On the evening of the 13th, an image of the Virgin is carried in procession from St Dominic's Church to the church on Penha hill. This is one of Macau's most important Catholic holidays.

June and July

Camões and Portugal Communities Day (June 10): In the grotto behind the Camões Museum (see p. 88), homage is paid to Luís de Camões, one of Portugal's greatest poets and author of the epic poem *Os Lusíadas,* which traces the history of Vasco da Gama's voyage to the Far East. The poet is thought to have lived in Macau in 1557.

Feast of St John the Baptist (June 24): Special masses are held in honour of Macau's patron saint. This day also commemorates Macau's victory on June 24, 1622, over Dutch forces who attacked the city.

Feast of the Battle of July 13: Only the islands of Coloane and Taipa celebrate this holiday, which commemorates their crucial victory in 1910 over the pirates that had infested the waters around them.

October and December

Portuguese Republic Day (October 5): This public holiday marks the birth of the Portuguese Republic in 1910.

Portuguese Independence Day (December 1): A public holiday, this commemorates the restoration in 1640 of a Portuguese king to the throne after 82 years under Spanish domination.

FOOD

As surprising as it might seem, the most renowned speciality in Macau is African chicken. The colony offers an astonishing assortment of cuisines, combining recipes from Portugal's former African colonies with Chinese and Portuguese cooking. All restaurants are open every day of the year, with the exception of two or three days following Chinese New Year. For more information, pick up the **Macau Government Tourist Office's** booklet, *Eating Out in Macau.*

Map coordinates refer to the map, p. 70.

The price brackets for Macau restaurants are given below as guidelines only. The cost of a meal will obviously vary depending on what you order.

(E) Expensive   130 *patacas* and up

(M) Moderate   50-130 *patacas*

(I) Inexpensive 50 *patacas* or less

Chinese

Four Five Six (M), Lisboa Hotel (B2), ☎ 77666. Delicious Shanghai cuisine. Open 11am-1am.

Fu Wa (M), 11-13 Rua Dr Pedro José Lobo (B2), ☎ 76456. *Dim sum* (see p. 25) served at lunchtime.

Lee Hong Kee (M), 35 Rua da Caldeira (A2), ☎ 76670. This Cantonese restaurant specializes in seafood dishes.

New Palace Restaurant (Floating Casino) (E), Rua das Lorchas (A2), ☎ 574480. Cantonese cooking and *dim sum.* Open daily 6am-11:30pm.

Pun Kai (M), 44 Rua da Praia Grande (B3), ☎ 75934. Cantonese cuisine. Open daily 11am-midnight.

Tai Sum Un (M), 41 Rua da Caldeira (A2), ☎ 76596.

Tsui Hang Chun (I), 11-B Rua da Praia Grande (B3), ☎ 81618. *Dim sum* served at lunchtime. Open daily 7am-midnight.

Portuguese

Fat Siu Lau (E), Rua da Felicidade (A2), ☎ 573585. The most famous roast pigeon in Macau is served here. Open daily noon-1:30am.

Henry's Gallery (M), 4 Avenida da República (A3), ☎ 76207. Specialities include African chicken and huge prawns. Open daily 11am-11pm.

Pinocchio (M), 4 Rua do Sol, Taipa Island, ☎ 27128. Specialities include roast quail, spicy crab and pork. Open daily noon-11:30pm.

Português (M), 16 Rua do Campo (B2), ☎ 754455. Excellent Portuguese pork chops and pepper steak. Open daily 11am-1am.

Solmar (M), 11 Rua Praia Grande (B3), ☎ 74391. Specialities include chicken and fish soufflé. This restaurant is a meeting place for the Portuguese community of Macau. Open daily 11am-10:30pm.

▬▬ *GAMBLING*

Visiting Macau without going to a casino seems almost unthinkable. Many visitors, especially from Hong Kong where gambling is illegal, come here specifically to gamble. You can lose your last cent, win a fortune or simply observe this captivating universe at any hour of the day or night: most casinos are open 24 hours a day, seven days a week.

The smartest casinos are the **Lisboa,** the **Jai Alai Palace** and **Macau Palace (Floating Casino).** There are also numerous, less flashy establishments where the local population play. Gambling fever is everywhere, manifested in those distracted intense gazes focused on a pile of chips. Most hallways are lined with slot-machines known as 'hungry tigers'. The government has put out a guide explaining the rules of the various games.

You can play baccarat, roulette, black-jack (21) and boule: the rules here are the same as throughout the world. There are several specifically Chinese games: the most popular is *fan tan,* an ancient game using porcelain buttons. Another Chinese game, *dai-sui* (big and small), involves betting on big or small values appearing on a roulette wheel. The Chinese are, traditionally, frenzied and superstitious gamblers.

Also extremely popular among gamblers is jai alai. This sport—a sort of handball played with a long curved wicker basket—was imported by the Portuguese to the colony. It's worth attending a match, even if you don't participate in the betting, for the simple beauty of the sport. Most of the players are Portuguese. Matches are held at the **Jai Alai Palace** (B2) from Tuesday to Saturday in the evenings (from 7pm) and on Sunday and Monday afternoons (from 1:30pm). The **Estoril Casino** is in the same building.

Casinos

Lisboa, Avenida da Amizade (B2), ☎ 776666. The Lisboa is a veritable monument to gambling. Gamblers can find everything they might need without stepping foot outside. There's a hotel, restaurants, swimming pool, sauna, massage parlour, luxurious boutiques (to spend your winnings) and even a game centre for children (that functions with coins of course). The casino is spread over three floors and offers more than enough games to ruin an oil magnate.

Palace, Rua das Lorchas (A2), ☎ 574480. From a tourist's point of view, this casino—built out into the harbour—is by far the most interesting. The view of the junks and sampans is magnificent. On some afternoons Chinese opera performances are given in the restaurant. The Baroque decor ressembles a temple and, in a sense, that is exactly what it is. It recently added a horde of 'hungry tigers' (slot machines) to its battery of games and the chinking of coins echoes relentlessly in its halls.

LANGUAGE

While Portuguese is the official language, Cantonese is more widely spoken. In most places frequented by tourists, English is also spoken.

NEWSPAPERS (see Hong Kong section, p. 28)

NIGHTLIFE

Most tourists spend their nights gambling, often until the break of dawn. If, however, you've lost everything you're willing to lose or simply want to take a break, you can go see the **Crazy Paris Show**, a sexy cabaret performance at the Hotel Lisboa (B2; Avenida da Amizade, ☎ 377666). There are two shows nightly at 8:30 and 10pm, with an added performance on Saturday at 11pm. Also in the Lisboa, you can dance in the **Mikado** disco, or dine, dance and watch a floor show at the **Portos do Sol** nightclub (open daily 7pm-1am; floor show at 10pm). Other discos include the popular **Green Parrot** at the Hyatt Regency (Taipa Island, ☎ 27000, open daily 9:30pm-2:30pm) and the **Skylight** in the Presidente Hotel (B2; Avenida da Amizade, ☎ 553888, open daily 9pm-4am) which offers a great view and topless floor   shows.

Most Macau nightclubs have hostesses, usually Thai or Filipino. The most popular is the **Paris** in the Estoril Hotel (B2; Avenida Sidonio Païs, ☎ 572081). Among the other hostess nightclubs are the **Mermaid** at the Lisboa and the **San Fa Un Cabaret** (with a Cantonese floor show) at the Estoril.

ORGANIZING YOUR TIME

You can tour Macau and return to Hong Kong in a day, as many tourists do. If, however, you want to be more than a simple spectator, plan an overnight stay. Contrary to popular belief, Macau is not only out for your money. Before plunging into the fascinating world of casinos, take a walk along Avenida Almeida Ribeiro (the main commercial street), rummage around the antique shops, look over the border into China at Portas do Cerco, visit the Leal Senado and the Camões Museum, watch the junks and sampans in the harbour, relax on a beach on the island of Coloane, tour the city in a pedicab, enjoy a Portuguese meal prepared by a Chinese cook... and go back to Hong Kong feeling as if you had journeyed to a strange and distant land.

POST OFFICE (see Telephone section, p. 79).

SHOPPING

Macau, like Hong Kong, is a duty-free port. The selection of merchandise is certainly not as varied or abundant as in the British colony, but prices can be even cheaper since the overhead (shop rents and cost of labour) is lower. You can buy jewelry, antiques, porcelain, pottery, clothing and more.

The principal shopping area is along the Avenida de Almeida Ribeiro (A2) and on the narrow streets towards St Paul's between Rua dos Mercadores, Rua das Estalagens, Rua da Tercena and Rua de Cinco de Outubro (A2). Bargaining is accepted just about anywhere and you can expect discounts of about 10%.

Antiques and crafts

It is still possible to come upon genuine pieces from the Ming dynasty (1368-1644) and pottery from the Ching dynasty (1644-1912) in Macau's antique shops. Small pieces, including old jewelry and jade or ivory figurines, are sometimes smuggled across the border from China. Don't expect, however, to acquire antiques at rock-bottom prices. Genuine articles are expensive, while good buys are usually reproductions (often indistinguishable to anyone but a connoisseur). Most antique stores are located on Avenida Almeida Ribeiro and along Rua da Palm in the direction of the ruins of St Paul's (A2). In front of St Paul's, at Portas do Cerco, on Penha hill and on the streets around Rua das Estalagens, there are numerous small shops selling souvenirs and curios, porcelain, furniture, painted wooden sandals, bamboo bird cages and more. In some, you can watch the craftsmen at work.

Clothing

Clothing manufacturing is one of Macau's key industries and the shopper can expect to find 'made in Macau' clothes, especially knitwear, at bargain prices. Local factories such as Levis, Cacharel, Yves Saint-Laurent and many other name brands often dump their surplus or obsolete styles on the markets of Macau. The best places to pick up clothes at discount prices are at the street stalls of **S. Domingos Market** (B2)—open mornings—and on Rua da Palha or Rua dos Mercadores (A2).

Jewelry

Jewelry, especially gold, is undoubtedly Macau's most popular buy. Prices, indexed on the Hong Kong Gold Exchange, tend to be lower than in Hong Kong. To avoid falsification of carat value, the **Macau Government Tourist Office** and the **Goldsmith and Jewelers Association** have published a shopping guide, available at the tourist office on Travessa do Paiva (see p. 80), with a list of reliable retailers. Most jewelry stores can be found on Avenida Almeida Ribeiro (AB2). A label with the words 'Centro de Informação e Turismo Macau' is displayed in the recommended shop windows.

▬▬▬ SIGHTSEEING TOURS

There are numerous tours of Macau which begin in the city or are organized from Hong Kong. The Macau Government Tourist Office provides information on tours of the city and trips across the border to China. A typical city tour costs about M$60 to 70, including lunch, for a three-hour trip which covers the main sights: São Paulo, the Kun Iam Temple, the Floating Casino and the Jai Alai Stadium.

It is possible to book your tour in Hong Kong; this way, a guide will meet you on arrival in Macau. Consult the Macau Government Tourist Office or one of the licensed tour operators in Macau specializing in English visitors (many have offices in Hong Kong):

Able Tours, Hoi Kwong Bldg., Travessa do Pe. Narciso, Macau, ☎ 89798; 8 Connaught Rd. West, Hong Kong, ☎ 5-459993.

Estoril Tours, Lisboa Hotel, Macau (B2), ☎ 73614; Macau Wharf, Hong Kong, ☎ 5-591028.

Macau Tours, 9 Avenida da Amizade, Macau (B2), ☎ 85555; 287 Des Vœux Rd., Hong Kong, ☎ 5-422338.

Sintra Tours, Sintra Hotel, Macau (B2), ☎ 86394; 3rd floor, Shun Tak Centre, Hong Kong, ☎ 5-408028.

The Macau Palace, known as the Fl oating Casino, offers several floors of gaming rooms.

SPORTS

The **Grand Prix,** held on the third weekend of November, is Macau's most spectacular spectator sport. You'll need to reserve hotel rooms way in advance since hotels are filled to capacity. For Grand Prix information and bookings, contact the **Grand Prix Organizing Committee,** Leal Senado, Macau (B2), ☎ 556235. Other spectator sports include jai alai, and greyhound racing at the **Canidrome** on Avenida General Castelo Branco (races are held on Tuesday, Thursday, Saturday and Sunday evenings).

Many of the hotels have swimming pools and tennis or squash courts, often open only to guests and members. There are tennis and squash courts open to the public (daily 7am-10pm) at the **Mandarin Oriental** (B3; to reserve a court, ☎ 567888 ext. 3760). There is a public bowling centre at the **Hotel Lisboa.** Visitors can also use the sports complex on Coloane Island (see p. 90). For further information about sports facilities, contact the **Macau Government Tourist Office** (see p. 80).

TELEPHONE

Macau has long-distance direct dialling for international calls. Most hotels have telex and cable networks. Direct calls can also be made from the **General Post Office** on Avenida Almeida Ribeiro (A2) right off Leal Senado Square, from the central post offices on the islands and from all public phone booths. Local calls are free from hotels and cost 30 *avos* from public telephones. For directory assistance, call 5-73001.

TIME (see Hong Kong section, p. 37).

TIPPING

Most hotels and restaurants add a 10% service charge to the bill. If it isn't already included, 10% is the customary amount to leave. Don't be surprised if you find a 5% 'tourist tax' on your hotel bill—all but the smallest add this government tax.

TOURIST INFORMATION

The **Macau Government Tourist Office** is located at Travessa do Paiva (B2), ☎ 77218 or 75156. Pick up the indispensable *Guide to Macau* here.

Macau Economic Services, Rua Dr. Pedro José Lobo, 1-3EDF Luco Internacional, 5th floor (B2), ☎ 78211, provides information concerning Macau's industries and export possibilities.

TRANSPORTATION

Bike

You can rent a bike for next to nothing at the entrance to St Joseph College, Santa Rosa de Lima College or at the corner of Rua da Praia Grande and Rua do Campo (B2). Bikes can also be rented from the **Mandarin Oriental** and **Hyatt Hotels** (B3). If you choose to tour Macau by bike, you will be left with an unforgettable impression of its seven hills.

Bus

The city buses are an inexpensive means of transport. Street names are written in Chinese and in Roman characters and the city is small enough that, equipped with a map, you will have no problem getting around. The fare is 70 *avos* on all city routes. Buses run from 7am-midnight.

Moke

Visitors to Macau can drive themselves around the territory using mokes (small, jeep-like vehicles). There are two companies hiring out mokes:

Macau Mokes Group Ltd., ☎ 5-434190 (Hong Kong), 378851 (Macau); telex: 76444 MOKES HX; fax: 5-455626.

Avis Rent-a-Car, ☎ 5-422189 (Hong Kong), 555686/567888 ext. 3004 (Macau).

You can also book through the Macau Government Tourist Office.

Pedicab

A one-hour ride in a pedicab, a two-seat rickshaw propelled by a bike, costs between M$30 and M$40. Rates are negotiable and must be settled in advance.

Taxi

Taxis cost M$4.50 for the first 1 mi/1.6 km. There is a surcharge of M$5 if you want to visit Taipa and M$10 to Coloane. Few taxi drivers speak English, but they usually understand where you want to go.

MACAU IN THE PAST

L ong before the Portuguese came to Macau in the early
16th century, the port served as a shelter from typhoons for
fishing and trading vessels. The earliest recorded settlers were two
families from Fukien who arrived here towards the beginning of the
Ming dynasty (1368-1644). The area was then known as Ho Keang,
'Oyster-shaped Mirror', or Hoi Keang, 'Mirror of the Sea', since its
circular-shaped bay (now called Praia Grande) evoked images of a
mirror. Sometime around 1535, when the Portuguese first arrived
in the harbour, they found a shrine at the entry to the port
dedicated to A-Ma, the patron-goddess of the Fukien sailors.
According to local legend, A-Ma had rescued the crew of a Chinese
junk from a terrible storm. Grateful for her help, the sailors erected
a shrine in her honour. The first Portuguese settlers around 1557
called the area 'Povoação do Nome de Deus de Amação na China'
('Settlement of the Name of the God of Macau in China') or, more
simply, Macau, the Bay of A-Ma.

Portugal was the first European country to establish trading
settlements in the Far East. Only 15 years after the great
Portuguese explorer Vasco da Gama discovered the sea route to
India in 1497, the Portuguese began trading regularly along the
coast of China. With important outposts set up in Goa (India) and
Malacca (Malaysia), the Portuguese turned their attention to the
Chinese coast. After several fruitless attempts to establish commercial relation with the Chinese authorities, the Portuguese captain
Leonel de Sousa was granted permission to trade in South China in
1554. Temporary posts were set up in Macau, on Shanchuan Island
(south-west of Macau) and in Lampacau. Around 1557 (the date
usually given for the founding of Macau), the Chinese government
granted the Portuguese permission to reside in Macau. In return,
well-armed Portuguese vessels got rid of the pirates who infested
the waters in the area.

MACAU'S GOLDEN AGE

Macau soon became a flourishing centre of commerce, with the
Portuguese serving as intermediaries between Japan and China
(direct trade between the two countries was forbidden). In particular, Chinese silk was exchanged for Japanese silver. The Portuguese
also acted as agents for the Chinese, selling their goods throughout

the region in exchange for spices, shark fins, bird nests and other gourmet foods from the South Seas, cotton, indigo and ivory from India and wool, crystal and clocks (often musical, they were known locally as 'sing-songs') from Europe.

This was the Golden Age of Macau. Missionaries flocked here to spread the Christian faith, building convents, monasteries and churches, many of which still stand today. Macau soon became the centre of Christianity in Asia.

DECLINING PROSPERITY

Portuguese control of commerce in the region remained unchallenged for 70 years until the Dutch, Spanish and, finally, the British were attracted by the enormous fortunes being made. The Dutch began to develop their presence in the region (notably in Indonesia), unsuccessfully attacking Macau on several occasions between 1604 and 1627. The entry of these new trading competitors into the region brought about the beginning of Macau's decline. Then in 1639, Japan closed its doors to trade, delivering a serious blow to the Portuguese settlement. When in 1685 Emperor Kiang Hsi opened Canton to foreign traders from September to March, Portugal lost the last remnants of its commercial hold on the region. Macau, however, continued to serve as one of the major outposts for traders and missionaries.

In the middle of the 18th century, at the request of the Chinese, non-Portuguese merchants were granted permission to settle in Macau. Initially doubtful about the advantages of letting in British, Dutch and French citizens, the Portuguese soon benefitted from the situation: import taxes were levied on goods passing through, employment was created and new ties were established with merchants from Europe and Asia.

Macau's tenuous and already-dwindling prosperity disappeared completely when the British took over Hong Kong in 1842. Through the British East India Company, the British had already made significant inroads into commerce with China. Hong Kong became the new centre of trade and many Macau residents moved to the colony to earn their living.

A GAMBLER'S PARADISE

For the next century, Macau continued to survive on revenues from gold and opium smuggling, as well as several other small industries. Gambling, licensed by Macau's governor, Isidoro Francisco Guimaraes, in 1851, became—and remains—a prime source of income.

In 1849, seven years after China ceded Hong Kong to Britain, Portugal proclaimed its sovereignty over Macau. Originally contested by the Chinese, China never formally ceded the peninsula to Portugal but signed an agreement confirming Portuguese occupancy of Macau in 1887. It wasn't until 1951, one century after the British took over Hong Kong, that Portugal declared Macau a province.

After some unrest in 1966, including rioting and direct confrontations between the Red Guards and Portuguese troops, Portugal offered to return Macau to China but, fearing the loss of foreign revenue, China refused. In 1974, Portugal's new left-wing government again offered to give up Macau and once again they were turned down. Nevertheless, Portugal withdrew its troops and granted Macau administrative and financial autonomy as a 'Chinese territory administered by Portugal'. Finally, in 1987, Portugal and China signed an agreement stipulating that Macau will be returned to China on December 20, 1999. Like Hong Kong, it will remain a 'special economic zone' for a further 50 years.

MACAU TODAY

Macau is a Portuguese dependency on the southern coast of
China. It consists of a peninsula and the islands of Taipa and
Coloane and covers an area of 6.17 sq mi/16 sq km. The city of
Macau occupies almost the entire peninsula, which is 3 mi/4.8 km
long and up to 1 mi/1.6 km wide. Taipa Island is connected to the
peninsula by a bridge and to Coloane Island by a causeway. The
Portas do Cerco, an old stone barrier, marks the border between
Macau and the province of Guangchon in China.

Macau consists of numerous small granite hills, the most
notable of which are Penha Hill and Guia Hill, both still covered
with greenery. Most of the land, once covered with forests, has
been stripped for use in construction, although certain areas of
Coloane Island are being reforested. Land reclamation since 1912
has changed the shape of the peninsula, extending the harbour out
to sea. The highest point in the territory is Coloane Height
(571 ft/174 m) on Coloane Island.

ECONOMY

Except for fish in the Chu Chiang Estuary, the territory has few
natural resources. The major crops of the restricted areas of
farmland on the islands (only 4% of Macau is cultivated) are
Chinese cabbage, onions, lettuce and beans. Water is either
collected during rains or imported from China, which also supplies
Macau with food and inexpensive consumer goods.

Macau's major sources of income are gambling and tourism.
Despite the lack of an international airport, more than five million
tourists flock to Macau each year. Most are Hong Kong residents
who come on weekends and holidays to take advantage of
gambling, which is illegal in Hong Kong (of the 5,100,461 tourists
in 1987, 4,191,991 were Hong Kong residents).

Other key economic activities include the manufacture of
textiles, toys, fireworks, footwear, leather goods, artificial flowers
and ceramics. Textiles are the most important export product,
accounting for 70% of export revenues. Many textile manufacturers
began setting up factories in Macau in 1965 to avoid the import
quota restrictions Western countries had placed on Hong Kong
merchandise. The single largest export destination is the United

States, followed by Hong Kong, West Germany, France and the United Kingdom. Imports originate mainly from Hong Kong and China. Like Hong Kong, Macau is a duty-free port, but low rents and wages make prices here even lower than in the British colony, although the selection is neither as diverse nor as abundant.

GOVERNMENT AND POPULATION

Politically, Macau is administered by a governor who is appointed by the president of Portugal. There is an advisory council made up of five secretaries and the Commander of Security Forces, and a legislative assembly comprised of 12 members elected locally and five appointed by the governor. Police, sanitary services, public utilities, transportation and other municipal matters are handled by the Leal Senado (Loyal Senate), formerly the main governing body of the settlement.

Since the beginning of the century, successive waves of immigration have caused the population to swell from 74,866 inhabitants in 1910 to an estimated 433,000 in 1987. Immigrants flocked to the territory following the civil disturbances in China in the 1920s and thousands of refugees found shelter on Macau's neutral shores during World War II, raising the population to 500,000 when there was accommodation for only 200,000. Chinese immigrants fleeing the communists in 1949 placed a further strain on existing facilities. Since 1966, the government has stemmed the tide with a major crackdown on immigration, repatriating those caught entering the country illegally. The population density is as high as Hong Kong's, with almost 95% of its inhabitants living in the city.

The people of Macau are predominantly of Chinese origin (95%); only an estimated 3% are Portuguese. Yet, centuries under Portuguese rule and as a centre of Christianity have left their mark on Macau's appearance and its way of life. Chinese, Catholic and Portuguese national holidays punctuate the months of the year; Macanese architecture combines forms drawn from both cultures and adapts them to produce functional buildings particularly suited to the climate. Unlike Hong Kong or Singapore, Macau has miraculously managed to build sufficient housing for its residents and visitors without destroying its outstanding ancient heritage.

GETTING TO KNOW MACAU

It is possible to explore Macau in a day, but we suggest that you devote two or, better yet, three days to cover all the sites of interest at the leisurely pace that suits Macau's temperament.

▬ THE PENINSULA

Since it is only 3 mi/4.8 km long and not more than 1 mi/1.6 km wide, you can visit the whole peninsula of Macau on foot. Just wander about and you will inevitably encounter landmarks testifying to Macau's past. The following is a selective alphabetical listing of sites.

Dom Pedro V Theatre

Built in 1872, this is the oldest Western theatre on the coast of China. Located on Largo de Santo Agostinho (A2), it is not generally open to visitors, except during the performances which are sometimes given here.

Guia Fort and Lighthouse

Built in the 17th century, the Guia Fort and Lighthouse (the first lighthouse on the coast of China) is located on Guia Hill (B2), the highest point on Macau. It's a terrific vantage point for a view of all Macau (open daily 7am-sunset). There is a **chapel to Our Lady of Guia** in the fort but you'll need permission from the Macau Government Tourist Office (see p. 80) to visit it.

Kun lam Temple★

Built in the early 17th century during the Ming dynasty, this temple on Avenida do Coronel Mesquita (B1) is dedicated to Kun lam, the goddess of mercy (open daily sunrise-sunset). The first treaty of trade between China and the United States was signed here in 1844. The main stairway is guarded by two lions holding a ball in their mouths, all carved out of the same block of granite. According to popular legend, if you manage to turn the ball three times counter-clockwise, you are guaranteed a lifetime of good luck (it certainly doesn't cost anything to have a go before trying your luck at the casinos). Inside, you can use bamboo sticks to tell your fortune; the officiating priest will explain how it's done. The Kun lam Temple attracts many visitors and its ceremonial events are lavish. You can spend a good 30 minutes admiring the temple decor, its Ming-period porcelain, statues, gardens, etc.

Leal Senado★★

Considered the best example of Portuguese colonial architecture in the Far East, the Leal Senado (Loyal Senate) on Avenida Almeida Ribeiro (B2) now houses the Municipal Council of Macau. The main building was constructed

The imposing façade is all that remains of St Paul's Cathedral in Macau.

in the late 18th century; the façade dates from the late 19th century. The Leal Senado underwent complete renovation in 1972. Here you can see the celebrated blue-and-white Portuguese faïence and visit the fabulous public library (open Mon-Fri 9am-noon, 2-5:30pm, Sat 9am-12:30pm).

Lin Fung Miu ** (Lotus Temple)

Not far from Portas do Cerco on Avenida do Almirante Lacerda (AB1), Lin Fung Miu is, without a doubt, the finest example of Chinese architecture in Macau (open daily sunrise-sunset). Built in the late 16th century, it was used as a temporary residence for Chinese Mandarins visiting Macau. There are numerous shrines dedicated to various Buddhist and Taoist deities: the most interesting is the one dedicated to the gods of Arts and Social Sciences.

Lou Lim loc Garden

This garden, on Estrada de Adolfo Loureiro (B2), was modeled on the traditional gardens of Soochow (eastern province of China) and created by the rich Chinese merchant family Lou as part of its residence. It became Macau city property in 1974. It is a lovely landscaped garden with winding paths amid decorative 'mountains', a large lotus pond and grottos.

Luís de Camões Museum **

Situated on Praça Luís de Camões (A2), this building was the headquarters of the British East India Company in the 18th century. It is named after Portugal's renowned 16th-century poet, author of the epic poem *Os Lusíadas*. The museum exhibits a valuable collection of Chinese paintings and objects, including pottery of the Han and K'ien Lung dynasties, Ming-period bronzes and Ching-period porcelain. Unfortunately, it will be closed until 1992 for extensive renovation.

Behind the museum is Macau's oldest garden, the **Camões Garden and Grotto** * (there's a bronze bust of Camões here). The garden is popular among Macau residents for strolling, practicing *tai chi* and playing Chinese chess.

Ma Kok Miu Temple * (A-Ma)

Situated on Rua de Santo Tiago da Barra (A3) at the bottom of Barra Hill, near the entrance to the harbour, this 16th-century temple (open daily sunrise-sunset) is the oldest in Macau. It is dedicated to the goddess A-Ma, from whom the name Macau originated (see p. 81). The complex includes several buildings and sanctuaries dedicated to diverse Chinese deities. Illustrating the legend, a polychrome bas-relief shows a junk carrying A-Ma into Macau out of the turmoil of a typhoon.

Monte Fort **

On the hill overlooking São Paulo's façade (B2) is Monte Fort (Citadel of São Paulo do Monte). It was built by the Jesuits at about the same time as the church. In 1622, a year before its completion, the Dutch fleet attacked the Portuguese territory. The firing of one of its cannons (which luckily hit a Dutch vessel) was sufficient to drive them away. From Monte Fort (open daily 7am-sunset), there is a magnificent view of the city.

Old Protestant Cemetery *

This cemetery (open daily sunrise-sunset) on Praça Luís de Camões (B2) was the first plot of land purchased by non-Portuguese Westerners in Macau. They wanted to assure a resting place for Protestants who could not be buried in Catholic cemeteries. It was opened in 1814 and contains about 150 graves. Among the graves of seamen, traders and their wives are buried some of the people who made history in Macau and in the Far East in the 19th century: Robert Morrison, who wrote the first Chinese/English dictionary, began a translation of the Bible into Chinese and was instrumental in buying the cemetery; Captain Lord John Spencer Churchill, an ancestor of Sir Winston; Joseph Adams, grandson of the US president and more. Reading the inscriptions on the tombs is an instructive journey into Macau's past.

Portas do Cerco

Portas do Cerco, the gate between Macau and China at the northern tip of Istmo Ferreira do Amaral, was constructed in 1870. The words inscribed on the gate are from a poem by Camões and mean 'honour your country for it looks after you'. This used to be the place where people would come to look at the inaccessible land of China until China opened its doors to tourists. Now, the interest of the gate is symbolic. You can see communist China's soldiers less than 65.7 ft/200 m from the Portuguese flag and watch the incessant traffic over the border of trucks with Macau white license plates or Chinese yellow ones. You'll come away with a more concrete idea of the relations that have developed between the two zones.

Santo Agostinho (St Augustine's)

This Baroque church on Largo de Santo Agostinho (A2) was built in 1814. The statue of Our Lord of Passos is carried through Macau on the first Saturday of Lent (see p. 75). In the church is the **tomb of Maria de Moura,** a local heroine. She died in childbirth along with her baby soon after her marriage to the man she loved, who had lost his arm in a fight with another of Maria's suitors. She and her baby are buried here with her husband's arm.

São Domingos** (St Dominic's)

This 17th-century Baroque church on Rua do São Domingos (B2), built by Spanish Dominicans, is one of Macau's loveliest. The statue of Our Lady of Fatima is carried from here in procession during the Fatima festival in May (see p. 75). Its **museum** evokes the prosperity of the religious orders at the time of Macau's colonization. When services are not in progress, you can visit the church in the afternoon. Ring the bell on the gate by the main entrance.

São Paulo** (St Paul's)

Designed by an Italian Jesuit, São Paulo, on Rua da São Paulo (A2), was built in 1602 by Japanese Christians. It was almost entirely consumed by fire in a typhoon in 1835. All that remains is its splendid Baroque façade, Macau's most famous landmark, at the top of an imposing staircase overlooking the ancient quarter of the city. São Paulo was once considered the most important monument to Christianity in the Far East. Take a close look at the carvings and the bas-reliefs, where traditional Catholic iconography is combined with other images (Portuguese caravel plus Japanese and Chinese symbols).

Sun Yat Sen Memorial House

Sun Yat Sen, considered by the Chinese to be the father of modern China, was a doctor, philosopher and revolutionary. He was one of the prime movers in the Chinese Revolution of 1911 and the overthrow of the imperial Manchu dynasty. He became president of the first Chinese Republic and died in 1925. The house on Rua Ferreira do Amaral (B2, open Mon and Wed-Fri 10am-1pm, Sat and Sun 10am-1pm, 3-5pm) was built as a memorial to Sun, who lived and practiced medicine in Macau between 1892 and 1894. It contains numerous relics and photographs evoking his life and works.

THE ISLANDS

Until recently, the only access to Taipa and Coloane islands was by ferry. Now a bridge links Taipa to the peninsula of Macau and a causeway connects the two islands. You can get here by taxi or on bus n° 21, which runs along Avenida Almeida Ribeiro—with a stop in front of the Lisboa Hotel (B3). Otherwise, there are regular ferries to the major island villages from Outlying Islands Ferry Pier, opposite the Ma Kok Miu Temple, Rua do Almirante Sergio (A3).

Taipa *

Of the two islands, Taipa is the closest to the peninsula. Here, Portuguese architecture blends with the Chinese countryside; the traditional maze of shops and houses co-exists with modern air-conditioned buildings. Its 10,000 inhabitants live in four villages. The main economic activity of the island is the manufacture of fireworks (a dangerous job carried out in factories where security precautions are often minimal). There are also several textile and electronics factories.

The island has some unspoiled countryside, beaches (crowded in summer) and pine forests that are perfect for a relaxing walk. In the village of Taipa, there is a **Tin Hau Temple** built in the early 19th century. Nearby, on a cliff overlooking the sea, the **Taoist United Chinese Cemetery** is guarded by a 9.86 ft/30 m high statue of Tou Tei, god of the earth.

The **Taipa Folk Museum** (Cąsa Museu), on the Taipa Praia, is a colonial-style building where Portuguese family life in Macau at the beginning of the 20th century is re-created. This is the first building to be completed as part of a projected cultural centre.

Coloane *

Coloane, the larger of the two islands, is farther south. From its south-western tip (the village of **Lo Wan**), you can see the Chinese island of **Dahenqin** only 65.7 ft/200 m away. Coloane was once a well-known den of pirates, who were a constant menace to voyagers in the surrounding waters up until the beginning of this century. In Coloane village, a **monument** outside the **Chapel of St Francis** commemorates the decisive victory over the pirates in 1910. The chapel was built in 1928 and contains the arm bone of St Francis Xavier, who died in 1552 not far from Macau, as well as bones of various Christian martyrs of the Far East killed in the 17th century.

Today, fishing and farming are the principal activities of the island's 8000 inhabitants. Tourism has developed over the years, as a result of the island's lovely beaches, particularly **Cheoc Van** and **Hak Sa** (Black Sands). Hak Sa has a giant sports complex (open daily 9am-10pm), complete with an Olympic-size swimming pool, a roller-skating rink, a miniature golf course, a sports field and a children's playground. On Cheoc Van, there is a lovely inn, Pousada de Coloane (Praia de Cheoc Van, ☎ 28144, from Hong Kong, ☎ 28144), with a pool and restaurant.

Not far from Coloane village is **Coloane Park** (open daily 9am-7pm). It has quite a variety of local fauna, a walk-in aviary with numerous species of exotic birds, Chinese-style pavilions and a picnic area.

INTRODUCTION TO SINGAPORE

Singaporeans like to call their country 'Instant Asia'. No other society in the world contains such a mosaic of peoples and cultures. Singaporeans are Chinese, Malay, Indian, Indonesian and Thai. They are Buddhist, Taoist, Confucian, Moslem, Christian and Hindu. They have four official languages—Malay, Mandarin, Tamil and English—but they also speak Cantonese, Amoy, Hokkien, Teochew, Hainanais, Hakka, Foochow, Telugu, Punjabi, Hindi, Javanese and more.

Here, you can enjoy an unimaginable variety of cuisines from every region of Asia. You can buy fabrics from India, silks from China, batiks from Indonesia, pewter from Malaya, jade from Burma and an enormous range of high-tech goods from Japan, Europe and the United States—all at duty-free prices.

You can pray in the Hokkien Thian Hock Keng Temple, the Sultan Mosque, St Andrew's Cathedral, the Buddhist Temple of One Thousand Lights or the Hindu Sri Mariamman Temple. You can join in the festivities of the Chinese Monkey King's birthday, the Tamil festival of Ponggal, the Hindu procession of Thaipusam, the Thai water festival of Songkran, the commemoration of Buddha's birth or the Moslem Hari Raya Puasa marking the end of Ramadan.

On National Day, all of Singapore comes together to celebrate the birthday of the nation. Singaporeans—whether they're Chinese, Malay, Indian or other—consider themselves, above all, to be citizens of Singapore. They justifiably take pride in their country's achievements.

Since its independence in 1959, the former British colony has experienced an almost complete metamorphosis. From a slum-filled, poor and overpopulated developing country, it has become one of Asia's largest financial and trade centres. The standard of living is high, unemployment is low. Government housing has gone up while the birth rate has been brought down. The welfare system and medical care are good and the transportation and communication networks are efficient.

The visitor to Singapore will find its success inscribed on the façade of the city with its luxury hotels, modern offices, skyscrapers, multi-storey shopping centres and elegant boulevards. Despite this unparalleled urbanization, Singapore has deliberately and meticulously kept itself 'clean and green' (as one of the government campaigns put it). Parks and gardens dot the island, trees line the

---

Singapore in brief

Location: The island of Singapore is located at the southernmost tip of the Malay Peninsula.

Area: 239.7 sq mi/521 sq km. This includes the main island and 57 surrounding islets.

Population: 2,600,000 inhabitants, of which 77% are Chinese.

Capital: The capital city of Singapore spreads over 37.45 sq mi/97 sq km and contains three quarters of the country's population.

Religion: Buddhism, Taoism, Christianity, Hinduism and Islam are the major religions.

Language: Malay, English, Mandarin and Tamil are the official languages.

Political status: Singapore has been an independent republic since 1965.

Economic activity: Processing of petroleum and rubber; shipbuilding; manufacturing of electronics, pharmaceutical products and textiles.

---

streets and surround housing developments. Wherever there is a space, greenery is planted. Critics lament the destruction of the older quarters of town and the loss of ancient lifestyles but Singaporeans are generally proud of their 'Garden City'.

Take your time getting to know the many facets of this tiny island-state. Singapore is a society in transition, one of the most complex in the world, and it offers the tourist an enriching and impressive experience.

PLANNING YOUR TRIP

WHEN TO GO

Singapore lies immediately north of the equator. Daily temperatures vary little (64° F/23° C to 86° F/30° C) and there are practically no seasonal changes. Rainstorms can occur throughout the year, although they are more frequent between November and January, the first half of the monsoon season. It is constantly humid but sea breezes and the widespread use of air-conditioning make the climate tolerable.

GETTING THERE

Plane

Singapore, one of the major cross-roads of the Far East, is an ideal starting point for your stay in Asia. More than 10 million passengers pass through Changi International Airport each year, more voyagers than to any other country in the Far East. At least 40 of the world's major airlines fly to this small island, including Air Canada, Air New Zealand, British Airways, Japan Air Lines, Philippine Airlines, Singapore Airlines, Thai Airways International, TWA and United Airlines. Call them directly for reservations or contact your travel agent for further information concerning flights and organized tours.

Located on the east coast, 12.5 mi/20 km from the city, **Changi International Airport** was inaugurated on July 1, 1981. It is renowned for its elegant buildings and efficiency: in less than 30 minutes you can clear customs and immigration and pick up your luggage. There is a **Singapore Tourist Promotion Board** counter for hotel, excursion and transportation information and airport currency exchange offices are open around the clock. Expect to pay an airport tax when leaving Singapore: S$5 to Borneo and Malaysia, S$12 for all other countries.

Singapore Bus Service (SBS) links the airport to town. You can also take a taxi. No need to negotiate tariffs; the taxis are metred and the trip costs between S$13 and S$15. Do make sure, however, that the driver doesn't 'forget' to turn on the metre.

Ship

Only 6% of Singapore's visitors come to the world's busiest port by ship. This is partly because most shipping companies do not offer frequent and regular voyages. What's more, the cargo ships, even though they have passenger cabins, are not particularly well-equipped for travellers.

Road

There are several ways to get to Singapore from Malaysia. The roads are excellent and car rental is commonplace (Singaporeans take out special insurance when driving in Malaysia). You can rent a car in Penang or Kuala Lumpur and leave it in Singapore. You can also travel to Singapore by bus or collective taxi, notably from Kuala Lumpur (eight-hour trip) and Malacca (five-hour trip). Collective taxis can be hailed at the marketplaces. They are faster than the buses and only slightly more expensive. A bit of patience, though, will come in handy as you wait for collective taxis to gather their full load of passengers. Hitchhiking is another possibility; Malaysians enjoy meeting foreigners and will rarely pass a thumb in the air. It is important, however, to present a clean-cut appearance: shabby clothes and long hair on men are not appreciated here.

Train

There are five express trains daily between Malaysia and Singapore. The **Express KTM** takes six hours and 30 minutes between Kuala Lumpur and Singapore. A direct train links Butterworth (opposite Penang) to Singapore in 13 hours. The **International Express,** departing daily from Bangkok at 10:30pm, offers an extremely comfortable 37-hour trip.

ENTRY FORMALITIES

Passport and visa

You will need a valid passport to enter Singapore but regulations concerning visas are considerably relaxed for tourists. If you are a citizen of the United States, you can stay in Singapore for up to 90 days without a visa. If you hold a British passport, you will not require a visa at all. Canadian citizens can stay for up to 14 days without a visa.

Vaccinations

No vaccinations are required unless you are coming from an area infected with yellow fever.

Customs

Besides your personal effects, you may bring one bottle of alcohol, one bottle of wine and 200 cigarettes into Singapore. Permits are required if you wish to bring in arms, meat products, animals, plants or controlled drugs. Illegal drugs are very severely frowned upon in Singapore, as is pornography. There are no restrictions on the amount of cash, travellers' checks or foreign currency that you may enter with (or leave with).

MONEY

The currency unit is the Singapore dollar (S$) divided into 100 cents. Notes are in denominations of S$1, S$5, S$10, S$20, S$50, S$100, S$500, S$1000 and S$10,000. Coins are 1 cent (bronze), 5 cents, 10 cents, 20 cents, 50 cents and S$1.

All foreign currencies can be easily exchanged in any bank and travellers' checks and most credit cards are accepted everywhere. Bear in mind that while the standard of living in Singapore is one of the highest in the Far East, the cost of living is one of the lowest.

According to the most recent information provided by the **Singapore Tourist Promotion Board,** the average day's expenditure per person is S$244. Luxury hotels and expensive meals will obviously raise this figure, while a budget-minded tourist may spend less.

WHAT TO TAKE

Clothing

Singaporeans dress casually. Take a walk in the early hours of the morning in any of Singapore's residential districts; the women wear loose-fitting clothes, while the men lounge comfortably in shorts and T-shirts. For your own comfort, avoid synthetic clothes that tend to stick to the body, when it's humid. There's no need to burden yourself with lots of clothes; most hotels provide efficient and rapid cleaning services.

Women should bring light dresses, jeans and cotton or linen pants, shirts and T-shirts. A simple dress will do for evening wear. For men, a tie, and even a light jacket, can come in handy for fancier restaurants and nightclubs. Otherwise, pack sport shirts, jeans and cotton pants.

Medicine

'Clean', 'green', 'healthy', 'pollution free': these are familiar terms to the hygiene-conscious Singaporeans. Singapore is one of the few countries in the Far East where the tap water is perfectly safe (and fluoridated to protect children from cavities). The hospitals have such a good reputation that people from neighbouring countries come here for medical treatment. Do, however, carry a supply of any medicine that you are taking regularly since you may have difficulty getting what you need in local pharmacies.

Photographic material

There is no need to buy equipment before coming to Singapore. Any photographic material you've ever dreamed of can be found here. Film is available at very reasonable prices and can be developed in no time at all. Make sure that you have what is necessary to protect your camera against heat and humidity: waterproof wrappings and silica gel are advisable.

BEFORE YOU LEAVE: SOME USEFUL ADDRESSES

The **Singapore Tourist Promotion Board** is an extremely efficient and helpful organization that has many overseas offices, including the following.

Australia
Goldfields House, 1 Alfred St., Circular Quay, Sydney, NSW 2000, ☎ (02) 241 3771.

Great Britain
Carrington House, 126-130 Regent St., London W1R 5FE, ☎ (01) 437 0033.

United States
Suite 1008, 342 Madison Ave., New York, NY 10173, ☎ (212) 687 0385.
Suite 510, 8484 Wilshire Blvd., Beverly Hills, CA 90211, ☎ (213) 852 1901.

PRACTICAL INFORMATION

ACCOMMODATION

Singapore has an excellent network of hotels. Unfortunately, the choice of moderately priced and inexpensive hotels is limited. Rates tend to be fairly high, but they are negotiable everywhere except in luxury hotels. If you have not made advance reservations, you can make them from the airport at the Singapore Hotel Association counter. For an explanation of hotel categories, see Hong Kong section, p. 13.

Map coordinates refer to the map pp. 100-101.

▲▲▲▲ **Century Park Sheraton,** 16 Nassim Hill (A1), ☎ 7321122, telex: RS 21817 CPSSIN. Ultra-modern service in a classic English decor, only five minutes from Orchard Road. The hotel has an excellent Japanese restaurant. 461 rooms.

▲▲▲▲ **Dynasty,** 320 Orchard Rd. (B1), ☎ 7349900, telex: RS 36633 DYNTEL. This hotel offers grandiose luxury in a traditional Chinese style. Its architecture boldly blends the styles of a pagoda and a 1960s skyscraper. 400 rooms.

▲▲▲▲ **Goodwood Park Hotel,** 22 Scotts Rd. (B1), ☎ 7377511, telex: RS 24377 GOODTEL. The Goodwood is located a short distance from the central district but is easily accessible. Its old-style colonial ambience is full of charm and the service is impeccable. French, Chinese and Scottish restaurants, as well as a nightclub, swimming pool and boutiques. 235 rooms.

▲▲▲▲ **Hilton,** 581 Orchard Rd. (A1), ☎ 7372233, telex: RS 21491 HILTELS. Only 10 minutes from the city centre, this hotel combines the usual comfort of a Hilton with a French touch: Givenchy-decorated suites and nouvelle cuisine at the **Harbour Grill.** 435 rooms.

▲▲▲▲ **Hyatt,** 10-12 Scotts Rd. (B1), ☎ 7331188, telex: RS 24415 HYATT. This luxurious hotel has international restaurants, a swimming pool with bar and a nightclub that is one of Singapore's hot spots. 824 rooms.

▲▲▲▲ **Mandarin,** 333 Orchard Rd. (B2), ☎ 7374411, telex: RS 21528 MANOTEL. Well-situated and elegantly decorated, this hotel houses several restaurants (including a revolving one), five bars, fabulous tennis courts and swimming pool and luxury shops. 1200 rooms.

▲▲▲▲ **Marco Polo,** Tanglin Rd. (A1), ☎ 4747141, telex: RS 21476 BEDTEL. Right beside the **Tanglin Shopping Centre,** the Marco Polo is a bit of a walk from the central district. Gastronomic pleasure is guaranteed at its French restaurant; also a lively disco, swimming pool and shopping arcade. 603 rooms.

▲▲▲▲ **Marina Mandarin,** 6 Raffles Blvd. (D3), ☎ 3383388, telex: RS 22299 MARINA. This hotel is located on Marina Square, the new area that was built up on land reclaimed from the sea. Excellent Italian nouvelle cuisine in the restaurant. 640 rooms.

Singapore, one of Asia's busiest trade and shipping centres, has a distinctively Western appearance.

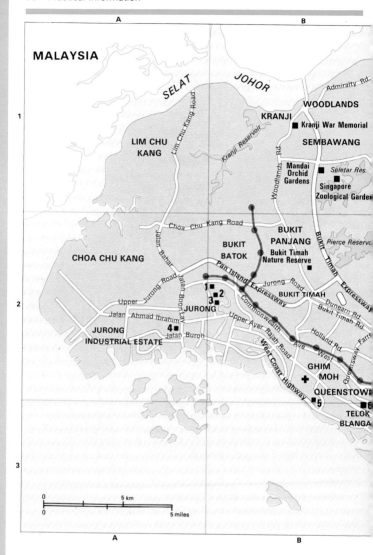

General map of Singapore

■ *Sites*

1. Chinese Garden
2. Japanese Garden
3. Singapore Science Centre
4. Jurong Bird Park

5. Tiger Balm Gardens
6. Temple of 1000 Lights
7. Botanic Garden

▲▲▲▲ **Meridien,** 100 Orchard Rd. (C2), ☎ 7338855, telex: RS 50163 HOMERI. Classic French ambience, including restaurant, brasserie and shops. 420 rooms.

▲▲▲▲ **Meridien Changi,** 1 Netheravon Rd., ☎ 5427700, telex: RS 36042 HOMRA. Situated 6.25 mi/10 km from the airport, this hotel offers the same comfort and standards as all the Meridiens. Free hotel/airport transfers. 280 rooms.

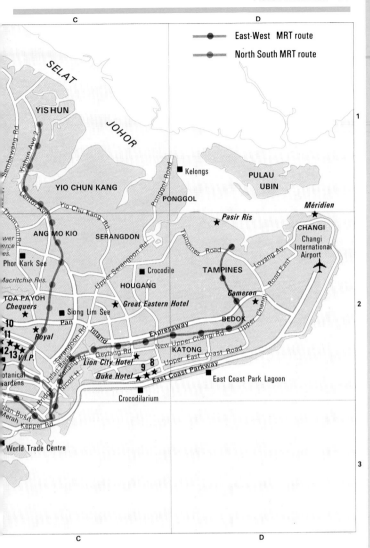

▲▲▲▲ **Ming Court Hotel,** 1 Tanglin Rd. (A1), ☎ 7371133, telex: RS 21488 MINGTEL. Personal and attentive service; Malay restaurant. 300 rooms.

▲▲▲▲ **Oriental Singapore,** Marina Sq. (D3), ☎ 3380066, telex: RS 29117 ORSIN. Associated with the renowned **Oriental** of Bangkok and the **Mandarin** of Hong Kong; 80% of the rooms look over the sea. 521 rooms.

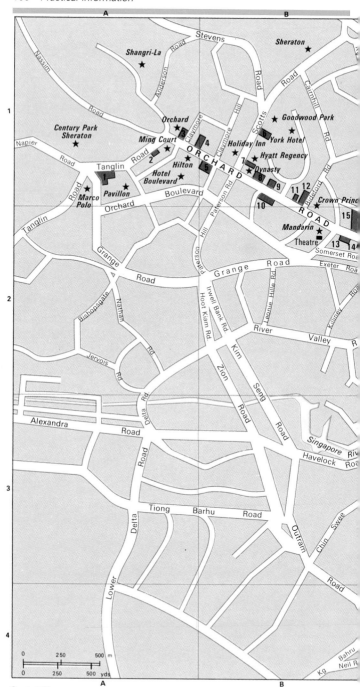

Central Singapore

★ *Hotels*

1. Singapore Handcraft Centre
2. Tanglin Shopping Centre
3. Delfi Orchard
4. Orchard Towers
5. Far East Shopping Centre
6. Far East Plaza
7. Scotts
8. House of Tangs
9. Lucky Plaza
10. Wisma Galadari

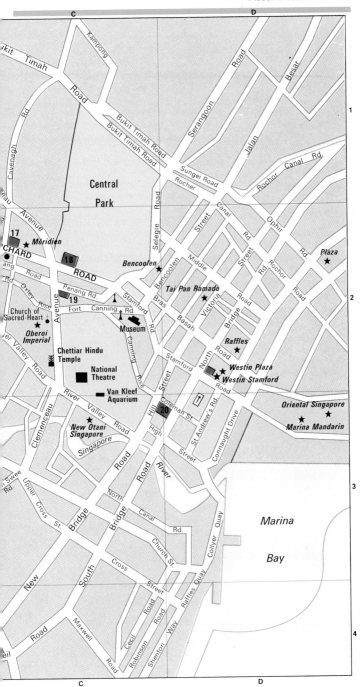

11. Promenade
12. Paragon
13. Orchard Shopping Centre
14. CTR
15. Centrepoint
16. Orchard Point
17. Meridien Shopping Centre
18. Plaza Singapura
19. Singapura Shopping Centre
20. Funan Centre

▲▲▲▲ **Pan Pacific,** Marina Sq. (D3), ☎ 3368111, telex: RS 38821 PPSH. An exterior elevator will speed you up the Pan Pacific's 37 floors in record time to the Cantonese restaurant. The lovely Japanese garden in the hotel is the largest outside of Japan. 800 rooms.

▲▲▲▲ **Pavillion Intercontinental,** 1 Cuscaden Rd. (A1), ☎ 7338888, telex: RS 37248 SINIHC. Globe-trotters who have stayed at the San Francisco **Hyatt** and the Hong Kong **Royal Garden** will recognize the same stunning architecture, with balconies overlooking an interior patio. It's worth a look even if you can't afford to stay here. 450 rooms.

▲▲▲▲ **Shangri-La,** 22 Orange Grove Rd. (A1), ☎ 7373644, telex: RS 21505 SHANGLA. This is Singapore's most beautiful hotel. It is situated in a splendid park complete with golf course, tennis courts and a swimming pool. Several restaurants, including Japanese, Cantonese and nouvelle cuisine. 700 rooms.

▲▲▲▲ **Sheraton Tower,** 39 Scotts Rd. (B1), ☎ 7376888, telex: RS 37750 SHNSIN. Excellent service; top-notch Cantonese restaurant. 429 rooms.

▲▲▲▲ **Westin Plaza,** 2 Stamford Rd. (D2), ☎ 3388585, telex: RS 22206 RCHKLS. Ideal for businessmen and conventions. 796 rooms.

▲▲▲▲ **Westin Stamford,** 2 Stamford Rd. (D2), ☎ 3388585, telex: RS 22206 RCHKLS. Listed in the Guinness Book of Records as the highest hotel in the world. From its restaurant, located on the top three of its 76 floors, you can see Singapore, Malaysia and Indonesia. 125 rooms.

▲▲▲ **Amara Hotel,**165 Tanjong Pagar Rd. (C4), ☎ 2244488, telex: RS 55887 SASHOT. Situated in the business district; television screens in its typically English club give constant updates on the stock market. 336 rooms.

▲▲▲ **Boulevard Hotel,** 200 Orchard Blvd. (A1), ☎ 7372911, telex: RS 21771 BOUTEL. Slightly off bustling Orchard Road, this hotel is centrally located and calm. The rooms are spacious and overlook a park. 528 rooms.

▲▲▲ **Crown Prince Hotel,** 270 Orchard Rd. (B1), ☎ 7321111, telex: RS 22819 HCROWN. Excellent seafood restaurant. 303 rooms.

▲▲▲ **Equatorial,** 429 Bukit Timah Rd. (C1), ☎ 2560431, telex: RS 21578 EQUATOR. Located near the university far from the centre in a lovely quiet setting. First-rate comfort. 224 rooms.

▲▲▲ **Glass Hotel,** 317 Outram Rd. (B3), ☎ 7330188, telex: RS 50141 GLHTL. The stunning architecture of this hotel includes an exterior made of glass. Houses Italian and Japanese restaurants. 509 rooms.

▲▲▲ **Holiday Inn Park View,** 11 Cavenagh Rd. (B1), ☎ 7338333, telex: RS 55420 HIPV. Located in the new commercial district; excellent Indian restaurant. 320 rooms.

▲▲▲ **Hotel New Otani,** 177A River Valley Rd. (C3), ☎ 3383333, telex: RS 20299 SINOTA. Built on the waterfront, midway between Orchard Road, Chinatown and the business district. The swimming pool overlooks Canning Park on one side and the harbour on the other. Excellent Japanese restaurant. 408 rooms.

▲▲▲ **Orchard Hotel,** 442 Orchard Rd. (A1), ☎ 7347766, telex: RS 35228 ORTEL. Conveniently located for shopping. 350 rooms.

▲▲▲ **River View Hotel,** 382 Havelock Rd. (B3), ☎ 7329922, telex: RS 55454 RVHTEL. Somewhat away from the hustle and bustle of the main avenues, this hotel offers excellent service. 476 rooms.

▲▲▲ **Royal Holiday Inn,** 25 Scotts Rd. (B1), ☎ 7377966, telex: RS 21818 HOLIDAY. Near many of the department stores, this hotel includes a miniature golf course, a rooftop swimming pool and German and Szechuan restaurants. 543 rooms.

▲▲▲ **Tai-Pan Ramada,** 101 Victoria St. (D2), ☎ 3360811, telex: RS

21151 TAIPAN. You can eat *satays* (beef, chicken or lamb skewers) at the pool. This hotel has several restaurants, a health centre and a business centre. 500 rooms.

▲▲▲ **York Hotel,** 21 Mount Elizabeth (B1), ☎ 7370511, telex: RS 21683 YOTEL. This hotel was completely renovated in 1987. Contains a Russian restaurant. 400 rooms.

▲▲ **Asia,** 37 Scotts Rd. (B1), ☎ 7378388. Situated in a quiet neighbourhood, this hotel has a good Cantonese restaurant. 146 rooms.

▲▲ **Cockpit,** 6-7 Oxley Rise (C2), ☎ 7379111. The accent here is on British-style tradition and comfort. Dress for dinner is jacket and tie. International, Chinese, Thai and Indonesian cuisines. 182 rooms.

▲▲ **Grand Central,** 22 Cavenagh Rd. (C1), ☎ 7379944. Located in a lively area of the city, near numerous hotels and shopping centres. Italian, Mongolian and Szechuan cuisines. 365 rooms.

▲▲ **Ladyhill,** 1 Ladyhill Rd. (A1), ☎ 7372111. The ambience here is Swiss. You can eat fondues in the **Le Chalet** restaurant. Nice rooms, large swimming pool, shops and attentive service. 174 rooms.

▲▲ **Metropole,** 41 Seah St. (D2), ☎ 3363611. Located near the Raffles Hotel, with a view of the harbour. Cafeteria and Chinese restaurant. 54 rooms.

▲▲ **Miramar,** 401 Havelock Rd. (B3), ☎ 7330222. Located near Chinatown, very comfortable. Contains a cafeteria open 24 hours. 346 rooms.

▲▲ **Novotel Orchid Inn,** 214 Dunearn Rd., ☎ 2503322. This hotel is 20 minutes from the city centre in a neighbourhood full of gardens and greenhouses. The swimming pool is surrounded by tropical vegetation. 321 rooms.

▲ **Hotel Bencoolen,** 47 Bencoolen St. (C2), ☎ 3360822. Situated in the commercial area, this hotel has a rooftop garden and restaurant. 69 rooms.

▲ **International House YMCA,** 1 Orchard Rd. (C2), ☎ 3373444. Right in the middle of the hotel district between Orchard Road and the Raffles Hotel, this YMCA offers a rooftop swimming pool, a fitness centre and tastefully furnished air-conditioned rooms. 121 rooms.

▲ **YMCA,** 60 Stevens Rd. (B1), ☎ 7377755. This YMCA offers impeccable comfort. 75 rooms.

AIRLINES

Air Canada, 100 Orchard Rd., 02-15 Meridien Shopping Centre (C2), ☎ 2355252.

Air France, 400 Orchard Rd., 14-05 Orchard Towers (A1), ☎ 7376355.

Air New Zealand, 10 Collyer Quay, 13-06 Ocean Bldg. (D3), ☎ 5358266.

American Airlines, 96 Somerset Rd., 03-01 UOL Bldg. (B2), ☎ 2353474.

British Airways, 14 Scotts Rd., 05-01 Far East Plaza (B1), ☎ 2535922.

Japan Air Lines, 16 Raffles Quay, 01-01 Hong Leong Bldg. (D4), ☎ 2210522.

Northwest Orient Airlines, 190 Clemenceau Ave., 03-29 Singapore Shopping Centre (C2), ☎ 3367666.

Philippine Airlines, 35 Selegie Rd., 01-10 Parklane Shopping Mall (C2), ☎ 3361611.

Qantas Airways, 333 Orchard Rd., 01-05 Mandarin Hotel (B2), ☎ 7373744.

Singapore Airlines, 77 Robinson Rd., SIA Building (C4), ☎ 2238888.

Thai Airways International, 113 Cecil St., 08-01 Keck Seng Towers (C4), ☎ 2249977.

TWA, 30 Bideford Rd., 02-00 Thong Sia Bldg., ☎ 7370700.

United Airlines, 16 Raffles Quay, 01-03 Hong Leong Bldg. (D4) ☎ 2200711.

▬ BUSINESS HOURS

Banks are open Monday to Friday 10am-3pm, Saturday 9:30-11:30am. Shops are usually open 9:30 or 10am-10pm, but Chinese and Indian merchants, in particular, tend to stay open late at night (some until midnight). Many stores are open on Sundays, though commercial activity is greatly slowed down. In Singapore, you can spend money at any hour of the day or night.

▬ CONSULATES

Australia, 25 Napier Rd. (A1), ☎ 7379311; open Mon-Fri 8:30am-noon, 2-4pm.
Canada, 230 Orchard Rd., 09-230 Faber House (B2), ☎ 7371322; open Mon-Fri 8am-12:30pm, 1:30-4:30pm.
Great Britain, Tanglin Rd. (A1), ☎ 4739333; open Mon-Fri 9am-noon, 2-4pm.
United States, 30 Hill St. (C2), ☎ 3380251; open Mon-Fri 8:30am-noon.

▬ CURRENCY EXCHANGE

Banks, hotels and licensed money-changers handle foreign currency exchange (cash or travellers' checks). Hotels usually add a service charge amounting to around 10 cents per US dollar. Money-changers, ubiquitous on Change Alley and around Raffles Place, often give better rates than banks or hotels.

▬ ELECTRICITY

In all hotels, the electricity is 220 volts. Most hotels will supply you with adaptors.

▬ EMERGENCIES

Most hotels have a resident doctor available around the clock. You can find doctors listed in the telephone directory under 'Medical Practitioners', dentists under 'Dental Surgeons'. There are 27 state hospitals (where health services are very inexpensive) in Singapore and several private hospitals. The major hospital addresses are:
- **American Hospital,** 321 Joo Chiat Pl., ☎ 3447588.
- **Gleneagles Hospital,** 5-6 Napier Rd. (A1), ☎ 4737222.
- **Mount Elizabeth Hospital,** 3 Mount Elizabeth (B1), ☎ 7372666.
- **Singapore General Hospital,** Outram Rd. (B3), ☎ 2223322.
- **Thomson Medical Centre,** 339 Thomson Rd., ☎ 2569494.
Some useful telephone numbers:
- **Police:** 999.
- **Ambulance, fire department:** 995.

▬ FESTIVALS AND PUBLIC HOLIDAYS

Singapore observes Chinese, Malay (Moslem), Indian and Western customs so holidays are celebrated and festivals are held throughout the year. Most holidays follow the lunar calendar. The following list is by no means exhaustive. For a complete listing and the exact date of festivities each year, contact the **Singapore Tourist Promotion Board** (see pp. 95, 116).

January and February
Thaipusam (Indian): In honour of the deity Lord Subramaniam, thousands of devotees converge on the Mariamman and Chettiar temples from mid-January to early February. Some practice self-mortification, piercing their

skin with metal hooks and carrying *kavadi* (a steel structure decorated with flowers, fruits, peacock feathers and pious images) on their shoulders. Others walk barefoot on glowing coals. In the evening, there is a procession in which the image of Lord Subramaniam is carried through the streets.

Farewell to the Deity of the Home (Chinese): On the eve of the Chinese New Year, the Deity of the Home goes to heaven to report to the Jade Emperor. For this occasion houses are cleaned and kitchens are scrubbed spotless. Formerly, the statue of the deity was smeared with opium so that she'd arrive in heaven in a state of euphoria.

Chinese New Year: Falling on the day of the full moon, around February, this is the most important Chinese festival and is the occasion to exchange good wishes. Children receive *hong bao*, little red envelopes containing 'good luck money'. Red, the symbol of joy, is everywhere. The Chinese tend to gamble on this day even more feverishly than usual, convinced that good luck on New Year's Day means luck all year round. Firecrackers have been recently prohibited but the festive atmosphere remains. On the first Sunday after New Year's the traditional **Chingay Procession,** complete with decorated floats and lion and dragon dancing, is held.

Jade Emperor's Birthday (Chinese): Crowds converge on the Giok Hong Tian Temple on Havelock Road to celebrate the Jade Emperor's birthday. A Chinese opera is performed in the courtyard of the temple and lanterns are lit in the doorways of houses.

March and April

Kwan Yin's Birthday (Chinese): The Chinese visit the temples dedicated to the goddess of Mercy (there is one on Waterloo Road). Childless couples, in particular, come to pray to her for the gift of a baby.

Songkran (Buddhist): This Festival of Water and the Thai New Year is celebrated April 13-15. Devotees make offerings of flowers, incense and candles in temples. The statues are sprinkled with water as a sign of purification. You can see the ceremonies at the Anada Metyarama Temple on Silat Road.

May and June

Vesak Day (Buddhist): The birth, enlightenment and death of Buddha are celebrated in Buddhist temples everywhere. The monks in saffron robes chant *sutras* (prayers) all day long, while lanterns and candles are lit to symbolize his enlightenment. The most spectacular ceremonies are held at the Kong Meng San Porkark See Temple Complex, Bright Hill Drive, and the Temple of One Thousand Lights, Race Course Road.

Hari Raya Puasa (Malay): This day marks the end of Ramadan. The Moslems don their national costumes and spend the day praying in the mosques and visiting friends and family.

August and September

National Day: All elements of Singapore's multi-racial society gather opposite City Hall on August 9 to participate in the carnival atmosphere of a parade that features paper dragons, traditional Indian and Malay dances, acrobats and orchestras.

Festival of the Hungry Ghosts (Chinese): According to Chinese tradition, the spirits of the dead leave purgatory to enjoy themselves on earth on the first day of the seventh moon. At the markets, offerings are made and Chinese opera performances are given.

Hari Raya Haji (Malay): On the 10th day of the last month of the Moslem calendar, those who have made the pilgrimage to Mecca (the men are known as *hajji*, the women as *hajjah*) go to Baitulla. This is celebrated with prayers in the mosques and at social gatherings.

Mooncake Festival (Chinese): This festival commemorates the overthrow of the Mongolian dynasty in China. Children are given multi-coloured cellophane lanterns. Everyone eats mooncakes, pastries filled with lotus nuts, red bean paste and salted egg yolk.

Deepavali (Indian): The Festival of Lights marks the victory of good over evil symbolized by the defeat of the demon Narakasura by Krishna. Friends visit each other and houses are decorated with oil lamps.

Christmas: Orchard Road lights up for three weeks around Christmas. In shopping centres, you can hear live choirs singing with the Christmas spirit at the equator.

▬ FOOD

In Singapore, you'll be eating with chopsticks, of course, but also with your fingers, which is an art in itself. You should bear in mind that the decor in many restaurants is unrelated to the quality of the food: cooks in small outdoor restaurants can be as good as those in grand hotels. Moreover, you can eat anywhere in Singapore without worrying about hygienic standards, which are strictly respected everywhere. Singapore offers such a variety of cuisines that it is impossible to describe each in detail. The following is a list of the more popular styles. It will be up to you to explore the subtleties of each cuisine.

Three price brackets are given as guidelines to Singapore restaurants.

(E)   Expensive   S$80 and up

(M)   Moderate   S$30-80

(I)   Inexpensive   S$30 or less

Chinese restaurants in Singapore offer you the chance to discover the regional cuisines of many Chinese provinces, including Canton, Peking, Szechuan, Hunan, Hokkien and Teochew.

Cantonese

Cantonese cooking is not very spicy. Dishes are often steam-cooked and ginger is omnipresent. Some unusual specialities: shark's fin soup, swallow's nest, roast turtle and *dim sum* (see p. 25).

Fragrant Blossom Restaurant (M), Holiday Inn Park View, 11 Cavenagh Rd. (C1), ☎ 7338383. Try the *dim sum* and chicken dishes. Open noon-3pm, 6:30-10:30pm.

Kirin Court (I), 20 Devonshire Rd. (C1), ☎ 7321188. Here you can find delicious stir-fried Cantonese dishes. Open noon-3pm, 6:30-10pm.

Spring Court (M), 291A New Bridge Rd. (C3), ☎ 2206431. Founded in 1933, this restaurant has an excellent reputation. Specialities include almond chicken, crab dishes and steamed prawn rolls. Open daily 11:30am-2:30pm, 6:30-10pm.

Pekinese

Noodles, rather than rice, are the mainstay of Pekinese cuisine, which is extremely elaborate. Peking duck is a speciality that is savoured worldwide.

Eastern Palace (M), Lucky Plaza Shopping Centre, Orchard Rd. (B1), ☎ 2357653. The ornate decor provides the perfect setting for a delicious meal. Open daily 11:30am-3pm, 6:30-10:30pm.

Jade Room (M), 290 Orchard Rd. (B2), ☎ 7372388. This restaurant features a 'greenish soup' presented in a fruit decorated with yin/yang symbols. Open daily noon-3:30pm, 6:30-11pm.

Prima Tower Revolving Restaurant (E), 201 Keppel Rd., ☎ 2220344. A stunning view of the city is offered with typical Peking dishes and *dim sum*. Open daily 11am-3pm.

Chinese residents of Singapore celebrate the New Year.

Szechuan

Szechuan dishes are highly spiced with hot pepper, garlic and soya sauce. The smoked duck is superb.

Dragon City (E), Novotel Orchid Inn, 214 Dunearn Rd., ☎ 2547070. Specialities include spare-ribs, Peking duck and shrimp with dried hot peppers. Open 11:30am-3pm, 6:30-11pm.

Golden Phoenix (E), Hotel Equatorial, 429 Bukit Timah Rd. (C1), ☎ 7320431. Specialities include shrimp in hot sauce and shredded chicken with red chili. Open daily noon-3pm, 7-11pm.

Min Jiang (M), Goodwood Park Hotel, 22 Scotts Rd. (B1), ☎ 7375337. Duck smoked with tea leaves and camphor. Open 11:30am-3:30pm, 6-11pm.

Hunan

Hunan cuisine is famed for its honeyed ham and pigeon soup.

Charming Garden (E), Novotel Orchid Hotel, 214 Dunearn Rd., ☎ 2518149. The Yunnan ham and diced pigeon are highly recommended. Open daily 11:30am-2:30pm, 6:30-10:30pm.

Hokkien

Hokkien cooking uses a lot of noodles (noodle soup, fried noodles, etc.) and can be found in most of the outdoor restaurants.

Beng Hiang (I), 20 Murray St., Food Alley (off Maxwell Rd., C4), ☎ 2216695. The decor is modest, but Beng Hiang, one of the few Hokkien restaurants, offers the best value for your money. Open daily noon-3pm, 6-10pm.

Teochew

The accent is on heavy sauces, Chinese-style fondues and gelatinous desserts.

Ban Seng (I), 79 New Bridge Rd. (C3), ☎ 5341471. This small restaurant offers specialities which include sea cucumber, goose and chicken on skewers. Open daily noon-3:30pm, 6-11pm.

Chao Zhou Garden Restaurant (E), UIC Bldg., Shenton Way (C4), ☎ 2256355. This is the best and most authentic Teochew restaurant in Singapore. Open 11:30am-2:30pm, 6:30-10:30pm.

Malayan

Malayan food is eaten with the right hand. It consists of lots of rice, surrounded by spicy meat, seafood and vegetables. The most well-known dish is *satay*—skewers of beef, lamb or chicken, marinated in a delicate blend of spices and grilled on charcoal. *Satay* is served with a sauce made of peanuts and coconut milk.

Aziza's International (I), 36 Emerald Hill Rd. (C2), ☎ 2351130. Good service and an agreeable decor accompany the speciality of the house, Malay oxtail soup. Open daily 11:30am-3pm, 6:30-11:30pm.

Nonya

Nonya, the cuisine of Straits-born Chinese (families which have been in the region for many generations, known as *babas*), blends the tastes from China and Malaya.

Bibi's Restaurant (M), Peranakan Pl., 180 Orchard Rd. (B2) ☎ 7326966. In the delightful dining room, try the soya specialities and coconut desserts. Open daily noon-3pm, 6:45-11pm.

Merlion Cafeteria (I), Orchard Towers, 1 Claymore Dr. (B1). Here you can find typical Nonya cuisine. Open daily 11am-3pm, 6-11pm.

Rasa Ria Restaurant (M), Goldhill Sq., 101 Thomson Rd., ☎ 2538349. Taste the mixture of Chinese and Malay cultures in the flavourful Nonya dishes. Open daily noon-3:30pm, 6-11:30pm.

Indian

There are more than 15 types of Indian cuisine available in Singapore. Curries, of course, are omnipresent but you can also find most of the specialities of North and South India.

North Indian

Dishes from northern India tend to be less spicy and more subtle in taste than their counterparts in the south. Curries are served with Indian breads such as *naan, chapati* and *paratha.*

> **Maharani (M)**, Far East Plaza, 35-36 Scotts Rd. (B1), ☎ 3393007. Here you will find a wide variety of Indian dishes. Be sure to tell the waiter how hot you want your food. Open daily noon-3pm, 7-11pm.
>
> **Omar Khayyam (E)**, 55 Hill St. (C3), ☎ 3361505. This is one of Singapore's nicer Indian restaurants. Open daily noon-3pm, 6:30-11pm.
>
> **Rang Mahal (E)**, Imperial Hotel, 1 Jalan Rumbia (B2), ☎ 7371666. Traditional Indian music accompanies the delicious food. Open daily 11:30am-3pm, 7-11pm.
>
> **Le Tandoor (E)**, Holiday Inn Park View, 11 Cavenagh Rd. (B1), ☎ 7338333. Delicious *tandooris;* Indian musicians provide a pleasant atmosphere. Open daily 11-3am, 6-10:30pm.
>
> **Ujagar Singh Jahal (I)**, 7 St Gregory's Pl., ☎ 3361586. This is an authentic place to try curry and beer. Open daily 11:30-3pm, 6-11pm.

South Indian

The hot curries of southern India are not for those with delicate stomachs. The best place to try them out is in the Little India quarter of Singapore.

> **Gopika Vilas (I)**, 5 Kerbau Rd. (D1), ☎ 3373130. For lovers of vegetarian food. Open daily 11am-3pm, 6:30-11pm.

Miscellaneous

There are restaurants in Singapore serving just about any type of cuisine from almost every country in the world—Russian, Japanese, Mexican, Italian, Korean, Spanish, Swiss, German, English or French. Western-style food is found mostly in the luxury hotels where the cooking is first-rate, the decor refined and the prices high. The following is a selection of several elegant restaurants in some of Singapore's biggest hotels.

> **Le Brasserie Georges (M)**, Hotel Meridien, 100 Orchard Rd. (C2), ☎ 7339955. Simple French cooking in relaxed surroundings. Open daily noon-3pm; 7-11pm.
>
> **Le Pescadou (M)**, Novotel Orchid Inn, 214 Dunearn Rd., ☎ 2503322. Southern French cuisine, with seafood specialities. Open daily noon-3:30pm, 7-11pm.
>
> **Le Restaurant de France (E)**, Hotel Meridien, 100 Orchard Rd. (C2), ☎ 7338855. Excellent cuisine; this is considered the best French restaurant in Singapore. Open daily noon-3pm, 7-11pm.
>
> **La Rotonde Brasserie (M)**, Hotel Marco Polo, Tanglin Circus (A1), ☎ 4747141. This is one of the city's best brasseries, with a welcoming, informal atmosphere. Open noon-3pm, 7pm-midnight.

Street vendors

Singaporeans eat at all hours of the day or night and just about anywhere. Raw meat, shell-fish, vegetables and so forth are served at stalls in the streets. You make your choice and the vendor will whip up a meal for you in no time. The following is a list of the places where you can find the best stalls:

Nighttime

Albert Street (C2).

Chinatown (C3).

Cuppage Centre (C2).
Newton's Circus (B2).
People's Park Complex, New Bridge Road (C3).
Rasa Singapura, Tanglin Road, near the Handcraft Centre (A1).

Daytime
Boat Quay (D3).
Capitol Shopping Centre (A1).
Cuppage Centre (C2).
Empress Place (D3).
People's Park Complex, New Bridge Road (C3).

LANGUAGE

English, Mandarin and Malay are the three most frequently used languages. Singaporeans also speak Tamil, Cantonese and other Chinese dialects. English is the main language spoken between different ethnic groups and between locals and foreigners. Most officials speak English, as do shopkeepers, doctors, taxi-drivers, hotel staff, etc.

MANNERS

Each ethnic group in Singapore observes its own particular customs. Despite their familiarity with Western manners, the Singaporeans are extremely attached to their distinct traditions.

● In private homes: Remove shoes before entering. This is customary with the Chinese, the Malays and the Indians.

● At table: The Chinese, of course, use chopsticks. The Indians and Malays use their right hand; under no circumstances should you use your left hand.

● In temples: Remove shoes before entering a mosque or a Buddhist temple. Don't wear mini-skirts, shorts or revealing clothes. You can take pictures but should ask permission first and it is customary to leave a contribution.

● With a camera: Certain Singaporeans will refuse to be photographed. Don't insist. Some people are superstitious and consider that taking a picture signifies stealing the subject's soul; others are simply modest.

NEWSPAPERS

The *Straits Times* and the *Business Times* are the two English-language dailies. The *Straits Times* publishes a daily listing of boat connections between Singapore and other Asian ports. There is also an English-language weekly, the *Sunday Times*. The Singapore Tourist Promotion Board publishes the *Weekly Guide,* which gives details of entertainment events. It is available free of charge in all major hotels.

NIGHTLIFE

When evening falls, the stores close and many of the major streets become deserted. Don't worry. Singapore's night scene is extremely lively but certain districts of the city are animated during the day, others at night. Here are some suggestions on how to spend an entertaining evening.

Dining under the stars

Singapore's street vendors, who used to trundle their 'restaurants' around the streets of the city, have been moved into permanent stalls in 'food centres'. The atmosphere remains informal and the food is good. Try out **Newton's Circus** (open until 2am). Make sure to ask about prices before ordering. For other addresses, see p. 109.

Despite Singapore's ultra-modern business facilities, there is still room for a public letter-writer.

Open-air Chinese opera

In the typical Chinese opera performance, a handsome and brave hero saves an innocent heroine from the evil scheming of a wicked lord. Whatever variations there might be on this theme, it always ends happily. Essentially, it is the unique atmosphere rather than the story that makes a Chinese opera so memorable. The costumes, makeup and sets revive an aspect of Chinese culture that transports the audience out of the world of concrete and skyscrapers. Free performances are given on the streets of the city. Whole neighbourhoods gather to watch. Operas are also staged during the day. Check *This Week Singapore* or *The Singapore Visitor* for details.

Cinema

Besides American movies (which you needn't come to Singapore to see), there are Malay, Chinese and Indian films, 'soya Westerns' and, of course, the extremely popular *kung fu* movies. Posters on the streets of the city announce current films, and newspapers publish complete listings. There are five screenings a day.

Amusement parks and roller-skating

Enjoy a Chinese-style amusement park, complete with games, rides and clowns, at **New World** on Serangoon Road and **Gay World** at Geylang (both open 6pm-midnight) or at **Singapore Wonderland Amusement Park** at Kallang Park (open 3-11pm).

You can go roller-skating at the **Golden Roller Skating Centre** of the Paramount Hotel, at 30 East Coast Road (open 10am-11pm).

Folkloric performances

In sophisticated surroundings, a cocktail in hand, you can watch Malay, Chinese and Indian dances, demonstrations of the Malay martial art *bersilat,* and other folkloric performances. These 'cultural shows' are presented in several places in Singapore.

Asean Night, by the pool of the Mandarin Hotel, 333 Orchard Rd. (B2), ☎ 7374411.

Instant Asia Cultural Show, Pasir Pajang Paradise Restaurant Theatre, Pasir Pajang Rd., ☎ 2352102. A 45-minute show of Malay, Indian and Chinese dances, snake-charming, lion-dancing and more.

Malam Singapura, by the pool of the Hyatt Regency, 10-12 Scotts Rd. (B1), ☎ 7331188.

Malayan Night Review, Raffles Hotel, 1-3 Beach Rd. (D2), ☎ 3378041.

Dining afloat

Dine on a boat that cruises the harbour between Singapore and the neighbouring islands. The cruise lasts approximately three hours. For information, see your hotel reception or contact a travel agency.

Nightclubs, discos and live music

Whether it's to pop, jazz or blues, the Singaporeans love to dance under bright lights. All the big hotels have a nightclub or disco. Among the more fashionable discos are: **The Rainbow** (A1; Ming Arcade, Cuscaden Rd., ☎ 7337140), **Top Ten** (A1; Orchard Towers, Orchard Rd., ☎ 7323077) and **The Warehouse** (B3; 322 Havelock Rd., ☎ 7329922). For other suggestions, look for nightclub ads in the daily newspapers.

For live jazz, check out **Saxophone** (C2) at 23 Cuppage Rd., ☎ 2358385.

▬▬ *ORGANIZING YOUR TIME*

Visitors rarely spend more than four days in Singapore. It's not much, but if you're an early riser, it's sufficient to get a grasp of the city. It's easy to get around Singapore rapidly. Strict regulations have facilitated and accelerated the flow of traffic. To organize your tours of each district, use a map published by the Singapore Tourist Promotion Board and available at any of its offices (see pp. 96, 116). All street names are indicated in English.

We suggest starting with a visit to the most well-known temples (they are also the most stunning), the aquarium, some marketplaces and the botanical garden. Watch an outdoor Chinese opera performance; take a walk through the jungle at MacRitchie Reservoir; give yourself a taste of what it's like to be a millionaire in the refined luxury of one of Singapore's grand hotels; dance to the rhythm of a Filipino band in one of the fashionable nightclubs; negotiate a ride on a trishaw (even if a taxi costs half as much); buy yourself a Japanese camera, an Indonesian batik, a Swiss watch, Chinese jades, a Burmese statue of Buddha, French perfume, Filipino shells, an Indian sari... Some claim that you can discover enough in four days to astonish you for a lifetime.

▬▬ *POST OFFICE*

The General Post Office is located in the Fullerton Building in the city centre. It is open around the clock. There are also many smaller post offices which are open Monday to Friday 8:30am-5pm, Saturday 8:30am-1pm. The post office issues aerograms and collector stamps. If you want to receive your mail by the general delivery service, it should be addressed to: Poste Restante, General Post Office, Fullerton Bldg., Singapore. Tell your correspondents to write your family name in capital letters to avoid confusion. Most hotels will post your letters for you.

▬▬ *SHOPPING*

A parrot with an American accent, your horoscope in Chinese, a made-to-order tweed suit ready in 24 hours, a stereo, orchids sent directly to your loved ones back home... a book could be written about all the strange and unexpected objects, Oriental or Western, to be found in Singapore.

As in Hong Kong and Macau, many items in Singapore are duty free; an attractive initial price may not, however, be the best deal. Don't forget that bargaining is the rule. The **Singapore Tourist Promotion Board** publishes extremely useful shopping guides available in all major hotels.

You can go broke, without even realizing it, by wandering around in the following areas:

Arab Street (D1-2): Handicrafts, jewelry, batiks and wickerwork from mostly Malay shopkeepers.

Change Alley (D3): Anything from toothpaste to a crocodile-skin bag. Entrance from Collyer Quay.

North Bridge Road High Street (D2): Camera equipment, fabrics, watches, leather goods from mostly Chinese merchants.

Orchard Road (BC1-2): Luxury boutiques, emporiums and shopping arcades in the grand hotels.

Raffles Place, Collyer Quay, Shenton Way (D3): Shopping malls.

Serangoon Road (D1): Handcrafts and jewelry from mostly Indian vendors.

Bargaining

Prices are fixed in department stores. Otherwise, bargaining is the norm and you should regard it as a necessary preliminary to buying. As a starting point, compare prices to get an idea of what an item is worth. The rest is between you and the shopkeeper. You can usually knock 15-20% off the original price and, if you're really good at it, you can get as much as 40% off.

Guarantees

Watches, cameras, electrical and electronic equipment, stereos, etc., usually come with one-year guarantees. Be sure they are valid outside Singapore; if not, you may be in for some unpleasant surprises when you get home.

Antiques

Antiques abound in Singapore: Ming-period porcelain, Sung (10th-century) ceramics, jade, ivory, Burmese and Thai Buddha statues, paintings on silk, ancient calligraphy, bronzeware, wooden sculptures. Chinese antiques prevail, but you can also find Thai ceramics and Indonesian masks and wooden chests. Most antique dealers are located on Orchard Road (BC1-2), Tanglin Road (A1), Raffles Place (D3) and in the big shopping centres.

Batik

Batik, a traditional Indonesian and Malay material, is sold by the metre (cut in pieces appropriate for sarongs) or as ready-to-wear clothing. Most patterns today are printed by machine, the handmade process using wax being too lengthy and expensive. Nonetheless, the original designs and quality of the colours have been preserved in the manufactured material. Check out Arab Street (D1-2), the shopping centres and especially the Singapore Handcraft Centre (A1).

Cameras

Just about all the major brands are available in Singapore. Prices are at least 40% below those in Europe and North America. Compare prices before bargaining on North Bridge Road (D2), High Street (CD3), Bras Basah Road (CD2), Middle Road (D2), Orchard Road (BC1-2) and in the shopping centres.

Chinese emporiums

These shops sell merchandise 'made in China'. This is one of the few places where bargaining is not done: items are already very cheap. You can pick up all sorts of bric-a-brac, handcrafts, silks, lacquerware, wickerware, porcelain and more. They are located on High Street (CD3), Grange Road (AB2), New Bridge Road (C3; People's Park Complex), East Coast Road (Katong Shopping Centre) and Orchard Road (B1; International Building).

Electrical appliances, radio, stereo and video equipment

There are shops selling calculators, electronic alarm clocks, hair-dryers, irons and every major brand of audiovisual and sound equipment from the simplest to the most sophisticated. Make sure the voltage and the current frequency are the same. Compare quality and prices at shops in the following places: North Bridge Road (D2), Bras Basah Road (CD2), People's Park Complex (C3), Orchard Road (BC2-3), Multi Storey Car Park, Market Street and Plaza Singapura.

Handicrafts

At the Singapore Handcraft Centre (A1; open Mon-Thurs 9am-6pm, Fri-Sun 9am-10pm), you can see a demonstration of batik wax printing or ivory sculpting.

Watches

Purchase a watch that measures the pulse rate (Tissot), that resists water pressure to a depth of 164.5 ft/500 m (Rado) or that is designed for use by the blind (Enicar). Seiko, Omega, Rolex, Piaget and other major brands are available on North Bridge Road (D2), South Bridge Road (C3) and in the shopping centres. You might even want to buy an imitation of a prestigious brand-name watch from one of the numerous sidewalk vendors.

Miscellaneous

The range of goods is enormous: jewelry from Malaysia (Arab St.), India (Serangoon Rd.) or China (Chinese emporiums); gems (South Bridge Rd., People's Park Complex); leather goods, crocodile-skin or other (Stamford Rd., Middle Rd.); all kinds of textiles (North Bridge Rd., High St., Serangoon Rd., Katong Shopping Centre, Textile Centre on Jalan Sultan); wigs (at hairdressers or in shopping centres); rugs (Orchard Rd., Tanglin Rd.); made-to-order or ready-to-wear clothing (Orchard Rd., Selegie Rd., Coleman St.).

▬▬▬ SIGHTSEEING TOURS

A multitude of excursions are offered, ranging from a morning harbour cruise to an exploration of Singapore nightlife which lasts until dawn. Contact the **Singapore Tourist Promotion Board** (☎ 2356111); although they do not actually organize tours, they can recommend reliable licensed tour operators. Information and reservations are generally available in most major hotels. The list below describes just a few of the more popular tours in Singapore.

City Tour

This is an indispensable way to get an overview of fascinating Singapore. The three-hour trip costs S$20-22 and tourists are taken through the main sightseeing and shopping areas of the city, including: Chinatown, the Thian Hock Keng Temple, the waterfront, the Botanic Gardens and a drive up Mount Faber for a panoramic view over the city.

Harbour Cruise

Boats leave from Clifford Pier in the morning or afternoon for a three-hour cruise. A Chinese junk takes you around the harbour, offering a splendid view of the city skyline. The routes vary but most trips include a visit to one of the offshore islands. Day cruises cost S$20, night cruises S$33, including dinner.

Sentosa Island (see p. 138)

This tour includes the 10-minute ferry crossing to Sentosa Island, where you will visit the Maritime Museum, ride the monorail and walk around the old fortifications. The morning or afternoon tour takes about three to four hours and costs S$28. The return trip offers a spectacular view of the harbour and city skyline.

Cottage industries and craftsmen play an important role in Singapore's economy.

Trishaw Tour

Available daily at 7 and 9pm, this tour (S$35) takes you on a pedal-driven rickshaw through some of Singapore's most fascinating back streets and includes a walk around Little India and Chinatown.

▬▬ SPORTS

Spectator sports regularly held in Singapore include cricket, rugby and horse racing. The **Cricket Club** is open to members only, but you can watch cricket matches on the Padang (D3) on Saturday at 1:30pm and Sunday at 11am (☎ 3389271). There are also rugby matches held on the Padang, Saturday at 5:30pm. The season for both cricket and rugby runs from March to September.

There's a beautiful race course at the **Singapore Turf Club** on Bukit Timah Road in the Bukit Timah Nature Reserve (☎ 4693611). There are usually eight races on Saturday afternoons starting at around 2pm, but call to confirm. The **National Stadium** in the suburb of Kallang often presents international sporting events. The **Singapore Sports Council** (☎ 3457111) can supply you with information concerning international competitions, as well as bookings to these events.

Singapore's recreation facilities are many and leave nothing to be desired. Most of the big hotels have swimming pools, saunas and squash courts, and Singapore's sports centres are usually open to the public, though you should call in advance to make sure.

Bowling

The **Singapore Tourist Promotion Board** recommends five of Singapore's bowling centres: **Jackie's Bowl**, 5428 East Coast Rd., ☎ 2416519; **Jackie's Bowl** (B2), 8 Grange Rd., ☎ 7374744; **Kallang Bowl**, 5 Stadium Walk, ☎ 3450545; **Pasir Panjang Bowl**, 269 Pasir Panjang Rd., ☎ 7755555; **Plaza Bowl**, Textile Centre, Jalan Sultan, ☎ 2924821.

Golf

Golf is extremely popular in Singapore, where there are more than a dozen golf courses. Among those that are open to the public, on certain days at certain hours, are: **Changi Golf Club,** Netheravon Rd., ☎ 5451298; **Jurong Country Club,** Jurong Town Hall Rd., ☎ 5605655; **Sembawang Country Club,** 17 Sembawang Rd., ☎ 2570642; **Sentosa Golf Club,** Sentosa Island, ☎ 4722722; **Singapore Island Country Club,** Upper Thomson Rd., ☎ 4592222. There is also a 65.7 ft/200 m driving range at **Parkland Golf Driving Range,** East Coast Pkwy., ☎ 4406726.

Tennis

Tennis is another popular sport and the numerous courts tend to be crowded, especially at weekends. Among the best places to play: **Alexandra Park,** Royal Rd., ☎ 4737236; **Changi Tennis Courts,** Cranwell Rd., ☎ 5452941; **Farrer Park,** Rutland Rd., ☎ 2514166; **Singapore Tennis Centre,** East Coast Pkwy., ☎ 4425966; **Tanglin Tennis Centre,** Sherwood Rd., ☎ 4737236.

Water-sports

First-rate water recreation activities are available at the **East Coast Park** with its beaches, swimming pools and rental facilities. The intrepid can slide into the water on one of Singapore's two giant water slides: the Big Splash in the East Coast Park and at the **CN West Leisure Park.**

Wind-surfers (and lessons), sailboats and canoes are available at the **East Coast Sailing Centre,** 1210 East Coast Pkwy., ☎ 4495118. Water-skiers can rent a speedboat and equipment at **Ponggol Boatel,** Ponggol Point, ☎ 4810031.

Scuba-divers will find the waters around the main island and the islets a perfect site for exploration. Many of the sampans or pleasure junks available for charter at Clifford Pier or Jardine Steps have scuba-diving and snorkeling equipment aboard. For further information, call the **Singapore Club Aquanaut,** ☎ 7370673.

▬▬ *TELEPHONE*

Local telephone calls (within the city) are free, except from public phone booths, where you will pay 10 cents.

Dial **103** for directory information (operators speak English). You can make long-distance calls through the operator at your hotel, or look in the front pages of the telephone directory for the appropriate codes to dial direct.

▬▬ *TIME*

Singapore time is GMT + 8, which means that it is eight hours ahead of London, 13 hours ahead of New York and 16 hours ahead of Los Angeles. Add another hour in the summer (from the end of April to the end of October).

▬▬ *TIPPING*

Tipping is rare in Singapore. Most hotels and restaurants add a 10% service charge and 3% government tax to your bill. Chinese and Indian restaurants usually dispense with the 10% charge. You needn't tip taxi-drivers unless they have helped with your baggage or if you have asked for an exceptional service.

▬▬ *TOURIST INFORMATION*

The **Singapore Tourist Promotion Board** is extremely active in promoting tourism. They publish numerous brochures, maps, etc., which you can pick up free in most hotel lobbies. Their staff is friendly and very helpful.

Singapore Tourist Promotion Board, 36 Raffles City Tower, 250 North Bridge Rd. (D2), ☎ 3396622. This is the main office, which is open Monday to Friday 8am-5pm, Saturday 8am-1pm. There is another office at the Singapore Handcraft Centre on Targlin Road (A1), ☎ 2355433, with the same opening hours.

Some useful telephone numbers:

Taxi service (24 hours): 4525555, 2500700.

Automobile Association of Singapore: 7372444.

Road service (Automobile Association): 7489911.

International calls: 104.

Time: 1711.

Immigration Department: 3374031.

Weather: 5427788.

TRANSPORTATION

Bus

Using the public bus system is one of the best ways of getting a taste of local life. Crowding and mayhem are simply nonexistent in Singapore. On the public transport system, Singaporeans conduct themselves with perfect impassivity.

The Singapore bus system operates more than 2700 buses which run daily from 6am to 11:30pm. Tariffs vary between 40 and 80 cents, depending on the distance. Since itineraries are not indicated at bus stops, you will need to pick up a copy of the *Singapore Bus Guide* (available in bookstores).

A one-day or three-day **Singapore Explorer Ticket** allows you to hop on any of the red-and-white buses of the **SBS (Singapore Bus Service)** or the yellow-and-orange buses of the **TIBS (Trans Island Service).** When you buy your ticket (sold at all major hotels), you will receive a bus map with suggested tours of Singapore. To further facilitate tourist bus travel, bus stops near interesting sites are marked 'The Singapore Explorer'.

Car rental

Renting a car is a good idea if you are combining your trip to Singapore with a journey to Malaysia. Otherwise, driving and parking in Singapore for a foreigner can be difficult. There are numerous one-way streets and the local metre-maids, who seem charming in their straw hats, are no more lenient about parking tickets than those back home.

A copy of the *Singapore Guide and Streets Directory* is an absolute must for finding your way around the city by car. Remember that driving is on the left and speed limits are 30 mi/50 km per hour on all local roads and 50 mi/80 km per hour on expressways.

Drivers must be at least 20 years old and possess a valid international driving license. You can rent a car in Singapore and return it in Kuala Lumpur or Penang. Minimum daily rates are S$60, not including gasoline. Look in the Yellow Pages for a list of 'Motorcar Renting and Leasing' firms. Ask them to explain the use of parking coupons in the city and the airport.

Warning: restricted zone

The Singapore government has established a strict system to prevent traffic jams. Certain areas of the city centre are restricted to private cars: those carrying less than four passengers between 7:30-10:15am must pay a fee. Since these regulations went into effect, a spirit of solidarity has taken hold in Singapore: neighbours get to know each other in car pools, bosses pick up their employees, strangers meet by answering classified ads in the newspapers. If you want to avoid paying the entrance fee to the restricted zones, you can always join the movement by picking up hitch-hikers.

Ferry

Ferries to the islands (Sentosa, Kusu, St John's) leave from the World Trade Centre. There are also departures from Jardine Steps on Keppel Road. For a more unusual experience, you can visit the harbour and islands by sampan. They can be rented at the above-mentioned places; tariffs are subject to negotiation. The **Port of Singapore Authority** offers cruises in the harbour and to the neighbouring islands. Your hotel reception will be able to give you information on all these excursions; otherwise, contact the **Singapore Tourist Promotion Board** (see p. 116).

Taxi

There are more than 10,000 taxis in Singapore and you will have no problem using them. They are well-maintained; the motors purr, the bodies gleam and the metres run perfectly. Drivers are usually honest, but make sure that the metre is flagged at S$1.60 at the beginning of your ride and that the driver doesn't forget to switch it on. Be sure, as well, that the driver understands your destination before starting off. The following is a list of surcharges that do not show up on the metre: 50 cents for more than two persons (maximum allowed is four); S$1 for luggage placed in the trunk; S$2 to enter the 'restricted zones' at restricted hours with less than four passengers; S$3 for trips from the airport. Note that tariffs go up 50% from 1-6am. You can rent a taxi by the hour or the day: for information contact the **Singapore Tourist Promotion Board** (see p. 116).

Trishaw

There are still lots of trishaws in Singapore. Their drivers belong to the poorer segments of Singapore society and they rarely speak English.

The sidecars fit two, but it is not unusual to see entire families transported in them, or groups of children on their way to school. Locals manage to bargain down prices lower than the tourists can. Use trishaws in the quieter parts of town where there is less traffic and you won't be suffocated by exhaust fumes.

Walking

Singapore, with its numerous underground and elevated walkways, is not a city for the walker who prefers to wander off the beaten track (you can incur a S$50 fine for failing to cross the street at a pedestrian crossing). Yet, there are still areas where it is a true pleasure to walk: the Botanic Gardens, the arcades of the ancient Chinese town (C3), the shopping centres, along the Singapore River (C3), on the Queen Elizabeth Promenade, on Change Alley (D3) or in the markets of the Chinese town (C3). Everywhere the colours, odours and contrasts of Singapore come alive in a way that is not apparent at first sight. There are few people who still know how to take their time. Join them; you won't regret it.

SINGAPORE IN THE PAST

It is February 1819. Two men are standing face to face, one British, the other Malay. The Englishman, Sir Thomas Stamford Raffles, an official representative of the British crown, is delighted; he has just purchased the island of Singapore from right under the noses of the Dutch. The Malay is equally satisfied. He has lost an island but gained a throne because Raffles recognized him as sultan in place of his rival brother (whose sympathies for the Dutch interfered with Raffles's projects). In the deal, the British Empire gained 150 new subjects: Malay farmers and fishermen and a handful of Chinese living in houses built on stilts at the mouth of the Singapore River.

Thus began the modern history of Singapore as a colonial outpost. Earlier settlements in the region are believed to date back to 1299. Chinese and Malay accounts refer to settlements here from the 13th century on and there is archaeological evidence from the 14th century. Little, though, is known about these earlier periods.

Singapore came to the foreground in the wake of Western commercial rivalries in the Far East. In the 17th century, British attention was focussed on the control of India and the only other British outpost in the Far East was Bencoolen on Sumatra's west coast. As trade grew between India and China, it became increasingly necessary for the British to establish a base along the sea route between the two countries. In the late 18th and early 19th centuries, the British partially accomplished this purpose by taking over first Penang, then Malacca and, finally, Java. Raffles was instrumental in the conquest of Java and became its lieutenant-governor.

RAFFLES'S EFFORTS PROVE SUCCESSFUL

At 14, Raffles had worked as a clerk at the London office of the British East India Company. This self-educated and ambitious son of a sea captain was soon sent abroad. He quickly learned to speak Malay and versed himself in Malay history, customs and traditions.

Raffles was driven by a desire to establish a strong commercial British network in Asia based on British ideals of free trade. Deeply disappointed when the British gave up Malacca and Java to the Dutch in 1814 (in exchange for Dutch support against Napoléon in

Europe), Raffles searched for another outpost along the southern Straits of Malacca. He did so against the orders of his superior, the Governor-General of India.

In January 1819, Raffles landed at Singapore. One month later, British jurisdiction was established in exchange for an annual payment. The British government was at first concerned that Raffles's move would provoke Dutch anger. His superiors were by no means convinced that this tiny island covered with marshland was of strategic importance. Raffles, though, held firm and the Dutch, after prolonged negotiations, recognized British sovereignty over Singapore in the Treaty of London (1824).

A GREAT COMMERCIAL EMPORIUM

In 1826, Singapore joined Malacca and Penang as part of the Straits Settlements, and by 1832, Singapore's importance had grown so much that the governor of the Straits Settlements moved from Penang to Singapore. Singapore quickly became what Raffles set out to make of it—'a great commercial emporium'. In 1823, before Raffles left Singapore, he declared it a free port 'open to ships and vessels of every nation, free of duty, equally and alike to all'.

Immigrants—Chinese, Malays, Indians, Thais, Arabs and others—were attracted by the opportunities provided by Raffles's principles of free trade and equality before the law. In Singapore, the new arrivals gathered together in districts according to their region of origin with each community specializing in a specific trade.

The population grew rapidly from a little over 10,000 inhabitants in 1824 (at the time of the first census) to almost 82,000 by the end of the 1850s, when more than 50% of the population was Chinese, and 139,208 in 1881. Then, as now, Singapore possessed a magnificent natural harbour situated on a narrow strait through which much of the traffic between East and West passed. The north-east monsoon winds, which lasted six months, blew ships from China to Singapore and on to India, and the ships rode easily back during the south-west monsoon.

The invention of the steamship and then the opening of the Suez Canal in 1869 increased Singapore's importance as an *entrepôt* between East and West. Tin-mining and rubber-planting developed in the last decade of the 19th century and the beginning of the 20th in Malaya, then under British control. Singapore merchants and workers became increasingly involved in these industries, which thus contributed to its prosperity.

WORLD WAR II

On February 8, 1942, the Japanese invaded Singapore from the north. The British, completely unprepared, were forced to surrender one week later. The Japanese occupation was brutal. Much of the European population was crowded into Changi prison where conditions were extremely oppressive. The Chinese, especially those suspected of actively supporting China in the Sino-Japanese conflict, were a particular target. Thousands were rounded up and massacred in the first weeks following the invasion. The Indians, on the other hand, were encouraged to cooperate with the Japanese who, for their part, supported Indian nationalism.

By the time the British returned in 1945, the situation in Singapore was disastrous: malaria was widespread, much of the population was on the point of starvation, and squatter camps had cropped up everywhere. Moreover, the image of British invulnerability and supremacy in South-East Asia had suffered a fatal blow. Nationalism was on the rise here, as it was in other colonies after World War II.

THE STRUGGLE FOR INDEPENDENCE

In the decade following the war, Singaporeans increasingly exhibited their dissatisfaction with British colonial rule through worker strikes, student unrest and even rioting. The movement in Singapore was encouraged by the integration of Malacca and Penang into the newly independent Federation of Malaysia in 1957. Two years later, Singapore attained autonomy from Britain under the leadership of Lee Kuan Yew, a young Chinese lawyer and head of the People's Action Party (PAP).

Lee has been described by admirers as brilliant, calculating, imaginative, determined and willful. His critics describe him as ruthless. Born in Singapore, of Chinese Hakka ancestry, Lee studied law at Cambridge. He symbolizes perfectly the ambivalence of the elite of his generation, divided between Oriental traditions and Western capitalism.

In 1963, Lee led the country into the Far East Federation of Malaysia. The union fell apart within two years and Singapore was forced—much to the chagrin of Lee, a leading advocate of the union—to become an independent and separate sovereign state. Friction between the predominantly Chinese Singapore led by Lee (whose Chinese origin disturbed the Malays) and Malaya was the cause of the separation.

LEE: MASTER PLANNER
AND DOMINANT POLITICAL FIGURE

In the first parliamentary elections following Singapore's complete independence, the PAP received a modest majority. Following a massive crackdown on left-wing opponents, Lee's former communist allies from the period of anti-colonial struggle formed their own party. The spectre of communist 'subversion' has remained a constant preoccupation of the Singapore government. In the decade that followed, the PAP gained more and more seats in parliament. In the 1972 general elections, they won every parliamentary seat and have since completely dominated political life despite the nominal presence of opposition parties.

In September 1988, the PAP once again dominated the general election. Although, previous to the election, there had been much talk of Lee's stepping down, this did not occur. Claiming a mandate from the voters, Lee retains a firm grasp on the reins of power.

SINGAPORE TODAY

L ocated at the southern tip of the Malay Peninsula, Singapore covers 239.7 sq mi/621 sq km and includes 57 islets that lie in the surrounding sea. More than three quarters of the population reside within the 37.45 sq mi/97 sq km of the city of Singapore. The island is linked to Johore, on the Malay Peninsula, by a 0.75 mi/1 km long causeway on which there is a road, a railway and a pipeline that supplies the small country with water.

Much of the marshland that covered the island at the beginning of the century has been drained. The city is full of modern skyscrapers and high-rise public housing. Outside the city, there are now numerous industrial and residential complexes, many built on land reclaimed from the sea. There are also some rolling hills and green countryside with pig- and chicken-breeding farms as well as horticultural and aquicultural installations.

TRANSFORMATION INTO A MODERN SOCIETY

When Singapore became self-governing in 1959, its prime minister, Lee Kuan Yew, was faced with the daunting task of transforming an overpopulated slum-ridden backwater colony into a prosperous modern society. Its assets were its strategic location on the maritime route between East and West and, like Hong Kong, its great natural harbour. It had, already, a solid position in the *entrepôt* trade which Lee was to develop over the coming decades. Today, Singapore's port is the busiest in the world in terms of tonnage.

The prosperity that this small island-state has achieved is undoubtedly one of Asia's great economic success stories. Singapore's birthrate has diminished greatly; most of the population lives in adequate government housing; a vast program of industrialization has raised its standard of living to the second highest in Asia (after Japan). Here the water is safe, the food is sanitary, the streets are clean and dotted with trees and parks, health standards are high, medical facilities are excellent and corruption is practically unheard of.

Lee, speaking of the profound metamorphosis of Singapore's society, remarked that 'from a minor fishing village (it has become)

Thian Hock Keng, one of Singapore's oldest temples, is dedicated to Ma Cha Poh, goddess of seafarers.

the biggest metropolis two degrees north of the equator', and, in a rare demonstration of humour, he added, 'It is the only place so near the equator where people do not go to sleep after half-past two if they have had a good lunch'.

INDUSTRIAL GROWTH

The island is practically devoid of natural resources and is almost entirely dependent on Malaysia for its water. Less than one sixth of the land is used for agricultural production, in particular vegetables, fruits and livestock. The agricultural sector's contribution to the GDP has declined continually over the last 30 years: from 6% in 1961 to 3% in 1970 and less than 1% in 1985, when a mere 0.7% of the labour force was employed in this sector.

To diversify its economy, Singapore embarked upon a vast program of industrial development. Petroleum refinement, shipbuilding, chemicals, electronic apparatus and office machines are among the major manufacturing industries. More than one quarter of the labour force now works in the manufacturing sector, which contributed 24% to the GDP in 1985 and experiences average yearly growth rates of more than 10%.

Petroleum refinement is one of Singapore's key industries: crude petroleum is imported from the Middle East and the refined petroleum products are exported. Singapore has the third largest refining capacity in the world. This industry, though, has been hit hard by surplus petroleum on the international market and by the development of refining facilities in oil-producing countries. Singapore is also the world's centre of the rubber and tin markets.

INTERNATIONAL FINANCIAL CENTRE

Over the past decade, the government has promoted Singapore as an international banking centre. Foreign investors were attracted through a series of measures that included tax incentives and special banking facilities. The Stock Exchange of Singapore, the Singapore International Monetary Exchange (SIMEX) and certificates of deposit in US dollars have drawn international funds. Foreign reserves were estimated at S$28 billion in 1986, when the finance sector accounted for almost one quarter of the country's GDP and employed 8.5% of the population.

Twenty years after Lee Kuan Yew first took office in 1959, Singapore's GNP had grown from $643 million to $7 billion. By 1985, it had more than doubled to almost $18 billion. Despite this rapid and sustained growth, Singapore's economy remains dependent on international factors such as fluctuations in the price of rubber and the supply of petroleum.

GOVERNMENT: A VIRTUAL ONE-PARTY SYSTEM

Singapore's government is a parliamentary democracy based on the British model. The head of state is the president, who has nominal powers. The 79 members of parliament are chosen in direct, compulsory elections. They, in turn, select the prime minister.

Since 1959, Prime Minister Lee Kuan Yew and his People's Action Party (PAP) have held the reins of government. The PAP had 77 members in parliament in 1987 and continues to control parliament since its election victory in 1988. Opposition parties are weak, partly because Singaporeans are generally satisfied with the PAP's achievements but also because the government does not hesitate to use stringent methods to suppress dissent and criticism.

Among the many controversial measures taken by the government are the arrest and detention without trial of political opponents (referred to as 'Marxist revolutionaries') and the control of labour unions and the press, so that outright criticism is rare.

Though the government's authoritarian manner has been criticized, most Singaporeans follow Lee's paternal lead with a discipline that astounds Westerners. The Confucian tradition of filial piety and respect for authority has contributed greatly in maintaining Lee Kuan Yew's hold on the country.

Daily life is governed by strict rules: you can be fined for littering (even for dropping cigarette butts), jaywalking or disturbing the peace by making too much noise; traffic is limited to certain areas of the city at certain times. In addition, public campaigns to promote government policy are common and have been one of Lee Kuan Yew's most effective tools in transforming Singapore's society. A telling example is the nationwide campaign to control population growth. In the 1960s, Singapore was well on its way to becoming one of the most densely populated countries in the world. Since, the birth rate has dropped drastically—from 4.7 in 1965 to 1.44 in 1987—due to a widespread campaign launched by the government. The public was told that 'two is enough'; family-planning groups were set up; contraceptives, abortions and sterilizations were made available. These measures were accompanied by incentives to keep families small, such as making housing available to smaller families.

The campaign was so successful that officials are now worried that there will soon be a lack of tax revenues to support the aging population. Now the government is urging Singaporeans to have larger families and offering tax rebates and access to government housing for larger families as well as child-care support. Match-making services have sprung up, particularly oriented towards those with higher education, who, theory has it, will produce more capable offspring.

ETHNIC DIVERSITY

Lee's supporters claim that his autocratic methods of governing have been a necessary evil to achieve the objectives of a multi-racial society, political stability and a healthy and modern economy. Singapore has, to a considerable extent, achieved all three of the goals. These are no meagre accomplishments for this tiny island-state with no significant domestic market, continually threatened by regional upheavals and uniquely isolated: Singapore is virtually a Chinese enclave in the midst of a Malay world. Of its 2.6 million inhabitants, 77% are Chinese. Another 15% are Malay and 6% are Indian, and within each group are further linguistic, ethnic and religious differences, making conflict practically inevitable.

The majority of the Singapore Chinese are from South China: Hokkiens from Fukien province, Teochews from Szechuan and Hakkas from Guangchon. Each group has its own distinct dialect, though Mandarin (encouraged by the government) is used to overcome language barriers.

THE CHINESE CLING TO TRADITION

Chinese immigration to Singapore dates back to Raffles's arrival, when many came to escape the poor conditions and ill treatment of the Manchu dynasty. The succeeding generations of Chinese born in Singapore were known as 'babas' or 'Straits-born Chinese' (like those born in Penang or Malacca). They have developed a culture that is, to a certain extent, unique to the Chinese diaspora of the straits settlements.

Religious practices, whether Buddhist, Taoist, Confucianist or animistic, have largely survived exile and urbanization. The Chinese worship an extraordinary pantheon of divinities. Temples reputed to confer luck on gamblers are thronged with devotees. No important decision is made without making sure that the gods are favourable; no building goes up without consulting a Chinese priest as to its location, orientation and other details of construction; and almost every Chinese home contains a family shrine dedicated to its ancestors.

It is not unusual to see an elderly Chinese merchant checking the results of a modern electronic calculator on his antique Chinese abacus, for tradition holds firm in the Chinese community of Singapore. Yet, over the years, the links between Singaporean Chinese and China have weakened. While most ethnic Chinese can speak the language of their ancestors, many have difficulty reading it. The decision-makers of the country, those who mapped the course of Singapore's economic miracle, such as Lee Kuan Yew, frequently received their education in universities in Great Britain. They are intent on creating a society in which the particularisms of the immigrants will blend into a larger, more homogeneous society of Singaporeans—creating a new individual who will not stand in the shadow of China.

MALAYS: BETWEEN PAST AND FUTURE

The Malays make up a tight-knit community reputed to be remarkably hospitable. Malay, Singapore's national language in which the national anthem is sung, is their dominant language, though the group includes Indonesians who speak Javanese, Boyanese and other dialects.

Virtually all Malays are Moslem and, at regular intervals, the cry of the *muezzin* calling them to their daily prayers resonates

Small fruit and vegetable stands abound in Singapore's Chinatown.

throughout the city. Orthodox Malays tend to be fervent believers and strict followers of Koranic precepts. The severity of Moslem law may have been somewhat tempered in this easy-going tropical environment, but Singapore's Moslems still turn towards Mecca. The orthodox save money to make the pilgrimage, never eat pork, fast during Ramadan, know the prayers and can read them in Arabic, go regularly to the mosque and observe all the Moslem holidays.

Few of the traditional Malay *kampongs*—native villages where houses were built on stilts—remain in modern Singapore. Most Malays have been moved into high-rise government projects and the civil service is a popular profession in their community.

Urbanization and economic development have accelerated changes within the Malay community, as they have throughout the society. Malay youth have been seduced by the 'consumer society' and the 'underground culture' of youth throughout the world: many have let their hair grow beyond the length tolerated by the government (in another of its numerous social campaigns, posters indicated the acceptable hair-length and advised those with longer hair that they would be served last).

Even though the Malays were the original inhabitants of Singapore, and in spite of their presence throughout the region (South Thailand, Malaysia, Indonesia and the Philippines), they have never exercised a determining political influence. The first president of Singapore, Yusof bin Ishak, was Malay, but he never fought for his community per se, convinced as he was that becoming a prosperous Singaporean was better than remaining a poor Malay.

THE INDIAN COMMUNITY

The Indian community of Singapore includes Tamils (60%), Malayalis, Sikhs, Pakistanis and Sinhalese. Despite this diversity, the community is extremely unified; this is particularly noticeable during Indian holidays. Singapore has more than 20 Indian temples, all of which are frequented regularly.

The Indians were originally brought to Singapore by the British East India Company to work as forced labourers on the major roads, canals and public buildings (notably St Andrew's Cathedral). This first generation of immigrants was soon followed by volunteers in search of economic prosperity.

So far, Singapore's Indians have partially resisted the exodus towards high-rise housing; much of the community lives in the areas around Serangoon Road, Market Street, Tank Road and Chulia Street. You will find Indian shopkeepers, policemen, transport workers and money-lenders. The latter are *Nattukottaï Chettiars,* a caste of Indian money-changers from the Madras region of India. You can see them in their white *dhotis,* a simple strip of cloth wrapped around the waist, handling incredible sums from tiny offices set up along the sidewalks of Market Street. In general, the Indians remain singularly attached to India: yet while many will save money to make the trip, it is inevitably simply for a visit.

A HARMONIOUS SOCIETY

Among Lee Kuan Yew's paramount goals has been the creation of a harmonious multi-racial society. The government has tried to forge a nation of Singaporeans out of this mixture of ethnic groups and religious practices. Language has been one of the main tools used in achieving this objective. In 1978, English became mandatory in schools; Mandarin the principal Chinese language. Malay, the official language of Singapore, and Tamil could still be used but were no longer obligatory in schools. Today, English has effectively become the language of commerce and administration and the *lingua franca* between the different ethnic groups.

Accommodating different minorities in the same government housing project has been another tool in facilitating ethnic coexistence. Distinct ethnic districts have almost completely disappeared, replaced by apartment blocks where choosing one's neighbours is out of the question.

In 1985, an apartment was completed every 20 minutes as part of a state program to re-house those who lived in the old quarters of the city. Every time a new industrial complex is set up, it is preceded by the construction of a high-rise village complete with schools, nurseries, sports grounds, etc. As a result of this unprecedented program of low-income housing construction, 80% of the population today lives in high-rise apartments.

While these buildings are undoubtedly preferred by Singaporeans to the post-war slums, critics claim that runaway urbanism has shaken the foundations of traditional social structures. Recently, the government has become aware of the need to preserve its cultural heritage. Plans to demolish Chinatown were shelved and several districts of the city are now being restored.

For 29 years, Lee Kuan Yew has mapped the course of his country and led it into the modern world. Will his successor be as adept in walking that fine line between political stability and the dangers of autocracy? Will he be capable of balancing the need to create a Singaporean citizen with the desire to preserve the valuable traditions of each group, the richness of Singapore's multi-cultural blend? Will he, finally, know how to continue the momentum of economic progress that has transformed Singapore into a worldwide centre of finance, industry and trade? Today, more than ever, Singapore is a society in transition.

GETTING TO KNOW SINGAPORE

Concrete, asphalt and modernism are not necessarily what tourists to the Orient are looking for and, in Singapore, the picturesque is increasingly difficult to discover. Singapore is essentially characterized by its modernity. This is a reality that visitors cannot ignore, even if they haven't come here with the idea of contemplating factories and low-income housing projects.

Yet, there is no reason to bemoan 'days gone by'. Singapore deserves to be observed with a fresh eye full of respect and curiosity. Take a look at one of the housing developments (Queenstown, Toa Payoh, Kallang or Jurong are the best to visit). Visit some of the historical buildings and districts of the city that have escaped modernization.

Despite rampant urbanization, Singapore is also a great place for nature lovers. There are immaculate lawns, trees, shrubbery, parks and gardens just about everywhere in the city and around the island.

We suggest that you spend at least a day exploring the various districts of the city, another in the beautiful nature reserves and parks to the north and at least half a day visiting Jurong Industrial Town, its parks and gardens. Finally, the east coast and the islands are perfect for recreational activities and water-sports.

SINGAPORE CITY

When Raffles landed in Singapore in 1819 he found a tiny Chinese community, some Malays and a few aborigines. As Singapore developed, British merchants flocked to its shores, there was a further influx of Chinese and Malays and an Indian community developed, mostly from the convicts brought here by the British as forced labourers. To avoid racial strife, Raffles settled each community in separate districts: the British in the centre to the north of the Singapore River, the Chinese to the south and the Indian and Arab communities to the north and east of the British quarter.

Today, despite the razing of whole sectors of the city and resettlement of their inhabitants in housing blocks, these districts have retained a good deal of their original character. This is especially true of Chinatown, the best-preserved area of the city.

Start your tour of the city with Chinatown, followed by a walk along the Singapore River, a visit to Singapore's colonial heart and, finally, a ramble through the Arab and Indian sectors. You can also spend a full morning or afternoon shopping on Singapore's upmarket Orchard Road.

Chinese opera is an integral part of Singapore's cultural life.

Chinatown** (C3)

South of the Singapore River is the area of the city where the immigrants from China settled over 100 years ago, re-creating the ambience of the homes they'd left behind. Today, high-rise housing has gone up in part of the district and organized indoor markets have replaced many street stalls, but old Chinatown has not disappeared completely.

The main artery is South Bridge Road. Its picturesque side-streets are lined with typical old Chinese houses: from the windows the laundry hangs out to dry, while birds sing in their bamboo cages. In Chinatown, you can find gold jewelry and red wooden shoes, jade stones and a game of *mah-jongg,* brocades and herbal medicines. Craftsmen and merchants still practice their ancient trades: calligraphers on the sidewalks of Sago Street and Ann Siang Hill paint good-luck messages on red bands or write letters for the old or illiterate; on Smith Street, third-generation wood-sculptors are busy engraving images of divinities; paper replicas of clothing, houses or cars, destined to go up in smoke during funeral ceremonies, are constructed on Ann Siang Hill where you can also buy theatre masks and lion heads; stalls selling fish and flowers line Trengganu Street.

Don't miss a visit to the oldest of Singapore's Chinese temples, the Taoist **Thian Hock Keng Temple*** (Temple of Heavenly Happiness), at 158 Telok Ayer Street. The temple used to be on the waterfront before successive land reclamation projects moved the harbour several blocks east. Newly arrived Hokkien immigrants would come here to thank Ma Cha Poh, the goddess of the sea responsible for calming the storms and granting safe journeys. The main elements of the building (including the statue of Ma Cha Poh) were brought from China in 1840. Today, elderly Chinese come to meditate in this tranquil place pervaded by the smell of incense.

Another Chinese temple dedicated to the goddess of the sea is the **Wak Hai Cheng Bio Temple** on Philip Street. Built in the mid-19th century by Teochew immigrants, this too was once on the waterfront. The temple's roof is covered with beautiful tiny pagodas and human figurines.

Chinatown is also the site of several non-Chinese places of worship. The most outstanding is the Hindu **Sri Mariamman Temple***, at 242 South Bridge Road (open daily 6am-noon, 4:30-8:30pm). Constructed in 1827 by Narian Pillay, an Indian architect who arrived with Raffles, this is the oldest Indian temple in Singapore. Over the years, the Dravidian-style temple has been renovated numerous times, most recently in 1984. The result is impressively Baroque. Hundreds of polychrome images of deities embellish the building. The best time to visit the temple is during early morning or evening prayers, or during Hindu festivals such as the purification festival of Thaipusam (see p. 104), when devotees walk on burning coals.

Moslem places of worship worth visiting in Chinatown include the **Jamae Mosque,** at 218 South Bridge Road; **Al-Abrar Mosque,** on Telok Ayer Street; and **Nagore Durgha Shrine,** at 140 Telok Ayer Street. All were built by Indian Moslems in the early 19th century. The Nagore Durgha Shrine is a peculiar combination of Eastern and Western architectural styles with its Doric columns and Palladian doors, and its façade covered with typically Moslem decorative patterns.

At the edge of Chinatown, on Eu Tong Sen Street, is the **People's Park Complex.** The huge outdoor market that once covered this site has been moved indoors. This is one of Singapore's liveliest shopping and food centres.

Singapore River*

The hundreds of barges and sampans that once cluttered the banks of the Singapore River have been removed in the last phase of a decade-long river cleaning program. The government has decided, however, to preserve the old buildings along its shore and the river has become the favourite spot for water-sports and dragon-boat races.

From Chinatown, walk towards **Clifford Pier** (D3) along **Change Alley** with its bargain shops and Indian money-changers. From the pier, where you can take a passenger ferry or pleasure junk to Sentosa and the southern islands or along the Singapore River, you'll have a splendid view of the harbour dotted with boats as far as the eye can see. Walk along the harbour to the mouth of the Singapore River for a look at the golden **Merlion statue** (24.3 ft/8 m high). This is Singapore's national symbol—half fish, half lion—derived from the two ancient names for the island: Singa Pura meaning Lion City and Temasek meaning Sea Town. At Empress Place on North Boat Quay (D3), there is a **statue of Raffles** erected on the site where he reputedly debarked in 1819. You are now at the entrance to the former British district of the city.

Colonial heart * (D3)

The core of Singapore's colonial district is the **Padang***, situated between St Andrew's Road and Connaught Drive. It is bordered by the Cricket Club, the Singapore Recreation Club, the Supreme Court, City Hall (home of Singapore's government) and St Andrew's Cathedral. The Padang has been the site of many historic and sporting events. This is the centre for the celebrations and parade on National Day (see p. 105).

The **Cricket Club,** constructed in 1850, was the centre of British community activities. Today, it is open to members only. On the opposite side of the Padang, the **Singapore Recreation Club** was used by the Asian communities, who were excluded from the Cricket Club. The **Supreme Court** was finished right before the Japanese invasion, and the Japanese formally surrendered on the steps of **City Hall** (built in 1929). There is a **War Memorial,** north of the Padang, on Beach Road, to those who lost their lives during World War II.

St Andrew's Cathedral* was built by Indian convict labourers in the 1850s in early English Gothic style. An earlier church on the same site had been damaged after being hit twice by lightning. This Anglican cathedral has magnificent stained-glass windows reflecting a stunning array of blue, green and violet pastels on the white interior of the church.

Between High Street and the Singapore River, you'll find three other renowned vestiges of the British presence: the **clock-tower, Victoria Memorial Hall** and **Victoria Theatre.**

Behind the War Memorial, on Beach Road, is the famous **Raffles Hotel****, opened in 1886. More than just a hotel, the Raffles is a monument Princes, lords, sultans, film stars and numerous writers (among them Joseph Conrad, Rudyard Kipling, Somerset Maugham, André Malraux) have stayed here. The last tiger of Singapore, touched by the hotel's exotic charm, took refuge under its billiard table in 1902 (he had escaped from a circus). This 103-year-old hotel will be closed in 1989 for about two years for extensive renovation.

From the area around the Padang, you can head west on Coleman Street to the **Armenian Church*** at the corner of Hill Street. Built in 1835 by architect George Coleman with contributions from the small Armenian community, it is the oldest of Singapore's churches and has become a national monument; services are no longer held.

On Stamford Road is the **National Museum and Art Gallery**** (C2; the museum is open Tues-Sun 9am-4:30pm; the art gallery is open Tues-Sun 9am-5:30pm; ☎ 3376077). The museum presents a panorama of the art, ethnology and history of the region: original manuscripts of Raffles, ancient maps, Chinese bronzes, Nonya objects, musical instruments, Indonesian puppets, etc. You can also admire the fabulous 385-piece **Haw Par Jade Collection** assembled by the family of the inventor of Tiger Balm. The art gallery has contemporary works and numerous temporary exhibitions.

Opposite the museum is **Fort Canning Park***, Fort Canning Rise, Clemenceau Avenue (C2). Known as the 'Forbidden Hill' to the Malays, this was once the site of the ancient fortress of Malay kings. Beyond the neo-Gothic entrance is a **cemetery** where the first European Catholics in

Singapore (since 1820) were buried. Also in the park are the **ruins of old Fort Canning** and a sacred **Malay tomb** supposed to be that of the last king of Singa Pura. Recently, squash courts and a restaurant were built on the grounds.

Nearby is the Hindu **Chettiar Temple***, on Tank Road (open daily 8am-noon, 5:30-8:30pm). The original temple was built on this site around 1855-1860 by Chettiars, a caste of Tamils from the region of Madras (essentially pawnbrokers). It is dedicated to Subramaniam, the six-headed Hindu god. The current temple was completed in 1984. The gateway is 70 ft/23 m high. Inside, the ceiling is adorned with lotus flowers, chandeliers and 48 glass panels each illustrated with an image of a deity. The best times to visit the temple are in the early mornings, evenings and during festivals, the most sumptuous being Thaipusam (see p. 104) and Navarathri.

Returning towards the city centre, you can visit the marvellous **Van Kleef Aquarium****, on River Valley Road (open daily 9:30am-9pm). More than 4000 species of fish, coral and sea animals are on view in the aquarium.

Arab Street* (D1-2)

Arab Street is the main artery of the Arab section of the city as well as the name given to the district between Rochor Canal Road and Jalan Sultan. Its centre is the **Sultan Mosque***, on Muscat Street. This is Singapore's largest mosque, built on the site of an earlier mosque which was constructed in the 1820s with a grant from the British East India Company (during negotiations between Raffles and the Sultan of Johore). Today's mosque went up in 1928 with private contributions from Singapore's thriving Moslem community. Five times a day (at sunrise, 12:30pm, 4pm, sunset and 8:15pm) the *muezzin* call to prayer resounds through the streets which are dominated by the mosque's minaret and domes. Midday Friday (the Moslem sabbath) prayers, in particular, attract thousands of fervent worshippers.

Along Arab Street, North Bridge Road and on the side-streets around the mosque (in particular on Baghdad and Bussorah streets), you'll find a large selection of Indonesian and Middle Eastern merchandise. Stalls and two-storey shophouses lining the streets sell wickerware, Indonesian batik, jewelry, perfumes and Malay religious objects (prayer beads, *hajji* caps for pilgrims to Mecca, prayer mats, etc.). During preparations for the feast of Hari Raya Puasa at the end of the month of Ramadan (see p. 105), Bussorah Street is lined with stalls selling all kinds of traditional foods and pastries.

Another popular mosque in the Arab section is the **Hajjah Fatimah Mosque** on Java Road. The building was financed in 1945 by a wealthy Malay woman (Hajjah Fatimah), who is buried in the grounds.

Little India* (D1)

This is the old Indian section of Singapore. On its main artery, Serangoon Road, you can find every Indian product imaginable, in particular an enormous variety of glimmering fabrics and spices. Along Buffalo Road, there are shops selling saris, garlands, diamond nose-studs and hi-fi equipment, and many Chettiar money-lenders have booths on this street. There is a lively food market at the corner of Clive Street and Campbell Lane. You can eat in one of the Indian restaurants, many of which are vegetarian, and have your fortune told by a bird.

Two Hindu temples on Serangoon Road are worth visiting. The **Sri Veeramakaliamman Temple** was built in 1881 by Bengali workers and is dedicated to the goddess Kali, a ferocious incarnation of Siva the Destroyer's wife. The **Sri Srinivasa Perumal Temple** with a 60 ft/20 m high gateway covered with polychromed gods is a popular place of worship and one of the centres of celebration during the Deepavali and Thaipusam festivals (see p. 104, 106).

The **Buddhist Temple of One Thousand Lights*** (Sakaya Muni Buddha Gaya Temple) is also in Little India on Race Course Road (open daily 9am-5pm). This lavish temple was built by a Thai monk in typical Thai style. The

The ornate Sri Mariamman Temple, the oldest Indian temple in Singapore.

giant (45.6 ft/15 m) **Buddha** surrounded by hundreds of light bulbs lacks refinement, as does most of the decor. Yet what the temple lacks in beauty is compensated for by the fervour of the devotees who come to venerate the mother-of-pearl replica footprint of Buddha and the piece of bark from the tree of illumination. Naive frescos recount the life of Buddha. For a nominal fee, you can turn on the lights framing the Buddha statue.

Orchard Road (BC1-2)

Modern luxury hotels and well-equipped shopping centres line the 1.8 mi/3 km length of Orchard Road, Singapore's elegant shopping boulevard. The stores are chic and expensive, although goods are still 20-30% cheaper than in their country of origin. The more popular shopping plazas on Orchard Road and Scotts Road are: **House of Tangs, Far East Plaza, Lucky Plaza, Promenade, Scotts** and **Centrepoint.**

Take a break from shopping at **Peranakan Place,** at the corner of Emerald Hill Road and Orchard Road. This is a showcase of the Straits-born Chinese, or Peranakan, culture. You can eat in the **Nonya** (Peranakan for 'woman') restaurant and visit the **museum** (open daily 11am-6pm), where a turn-of-the-century Peranakan residence is re-created.

When you reach the end of Orchard Road, continue along Tanglin Road to the **Singapore Handcraft Centre** (A1), which is open daily 10am-10pm. You can purchase traditional crafts from 16 Asian countries and watch demonstrations by individual craftsmen.

Miscellaneous city attractions

Established in 1859 on 79 acres/32 hectares, the **Botanic Gardens*** on Cluny Road (open Mon-Fri 5am-11pm, Sat, Sun and holidays 5am-midnight) are among Singapore's loveliest gardens. There are English lawns and bracken, lotus-filled ponds, vines alongside jungle streams and exotic birds playing amid orchids, frangipani and hibiscus. Walking through the gardens is an enchanting experience. Come at dawn if you want to see the *tai chi* experts performing their slow-motion exercises. On sunny Sundays, you can sit on the grass and listen to a concert.

A definite must for those spending a Sunday in Singapore is the **Bird-Singing Concert***. Hundreds of specially trained and selected champions gather every Sunday morning at a coffee shop on the corner of Tiong Bahru and Seng Poh roads (AB3) to give a concert unlike any other you are likely to attend. Many are Malay birds (merboks are the most talented) and their owners regularly bring them here to measure their vocal qualities. The concerts begin around 8am and attract fans from every corner of Singapore. An annual bird-singing contest is held in July.

NORTHERN SINGAPORE

Singapore's well-merited reputation for beautiful gardens and parks is confirmed in the north of the island, where the visitor can spend a relaxing and exhilarating day visiting the MacRitchie Reservoir, Bukit Timah Nature Reserve, the Zoological Gardens and Mandai Orchid Garden. You can still see some of the few remaining Malay villages built on stilts *(kampongs)* in the northern region of Sembawang. Immediately north of the city is the satellite city of Toa Payoh and the marvelous Siong Lim Temple.

Bukit Timah Nature Reserve *

At this 148 acre/60 hectare reserve on Upper Bukit Timah Road, you'll find clearly marked trails crisscrossing the kind of jungle terrain that once covered the entire island of Singapore. You'll have a splendid view of Singapore here, from the island's highest hill (538 ft/177 m).

MacRitchie Reservoir

Not far from the city centre, off Lornie Road, near Thomson Road, paths have been laid down in the jungle surrounding the MacRitchie Reservoir. This is a popular place for jogging or strolling and, if you're lucky, you might run into a monkey.

Mandai Orchid Garden **

This commercial orchid farm, on Mandai Lake Road (bus n° 171), can be visited (open daily 9am-5:30pm). The sight of millions of blossoming orchids of every variety is fascinating. The garden covers 9.8 acres/4 hectares. In July, you can see the rare black orchid of Sumatra. There are 300 varieties; each is a masterpiece.

Singapore Zoological Gardens *

Situated at 80 Mandai Lake Road 12.5 mi/20 km from the city centre (☎ 2693411), this zoo is home to 1400 animals of over 140 species, including monkeys, tigers, elephants, giraffes, rhinoceri and more, all kept in environments reminiscent of their natural habitats. You can eat breakfast with an orangutan. The easiest way to get here is to take bus n° 171 from Queen Street or bus n° 137 from Toa Payoh.

Siong Lim Temple *

Financed by two wealthy Hokkien traders and constructed between 1898 and 1908, this Buddhist temple, at 184 Jalan Toa Payoh, is one of Singapore's biggest. It's built in a Pekinese style, with several courtyards and gardens. In the interior are thousands of ancestor portraits atop commemorative tablets. The temple, which is overshadowed by modern buildings, is a perfect place to meditate on the destruction of much of the city's heritage caused by Singapore's urbanization.

THE WEST COAST

The main tourist destination on the west coast of the island is the industrial zone of **Jurong**. This is Singapore's major industrial area with 400 modern factories, employing approximately 70% of the industrial workforce. Its developers, true to Singapore's 'Garden State' identity, created three magnificent parks in the zone: Jurong Bird Park, a Japanese Garden and a Chinese Garden. Jurong also has a science centre. For a view of the industrial town and surroundings go to the **Lookout Tower and Hill Top Restaurant** (open daily 11:30am-10:45pm). There is a fantastic wholesale fish market in Jurong which sells a couple of hundred tons of fish each morning (from 2-7am) to retailers across the island. On the way to Jurong, you can stop off at the Tiger Balm Gardens.

Bird Park**

The Bird Park, on Jalan Ahmad Ibrahim, has more than 3000 birds in its 49 acres/20 hectares of splendid natural setting (open daily 9am-6pm; ☎ 2650022). Magpies from Taiwan mingle with cassowaries from New Guinea and ostriches from Brazil. The main attraction is the giant walk-in aviary, with birds flying around its 91 ft/30 m man-made waterfall (the highest in the world). It's easy to take pictures of many of the less wild birds and there are daily shows presenting trained birds. You can listen to the birds sing over breakfast at the **Song Bird Terrace** (9-11am).

Chinese and Japanese Gardens*

Off Yuan Ching Road stands the gateway of the Chinese Garden (Yu Hua Yuan), beyond which there are pagodas, arching bridges, weeping willows by lotus ponds and bamboo groves. The Garden, on a 33 acre/13.5 hectare island, is a reproduction of the Peking Summer Palace (open Mon-Sat 9:30am-6pm, Sun and holidays 8:30am-6pm). You can take out a rowboat to explore the waters. The Japanese Garden (Seiwaen), at the same location, is the largest traditional Japanese landscape garden outside Japan (same opening hours). Its Japanese name means 'tranquillity' and suits this lovely 8.6 acre/3.5 hectare garden perfectly.

Singapore Science Centre

These exhibition halls, on Science Centre Road, are devoted to natural and physical sciences and also present aviation in a stimulating manner (open Tues-Sun 10am-6pm; ☎ 5603316).

Tiger Balm Gardens (Haw Par Villa)

Less than 6.25 mi/10 km from the city centre on Pasir Panjang Road, the Tiger Balm Gardens, created by the inventor of Tiger Balm, are often called a 'Confucian Disneyland' (open daily 9am-6pm). The gardens offer an amusing (if not artistic) voyage through the fantastic world of Chinese mythology, represented by hundreds of polychrome plaster statues.

▬▬▬ *THE EAST COAST*

The eastern part of the island used to be dotted with small Malay villages. Most have been demolished to make room for high-rise housing. In the suburb of **Katong** you can see some well-preserved shophouses, wealthy residential districts and housing developments. Some organized tours take you to visit **Changi Prison chapel,** built by the British in 1927. The Japanese interned some 70,000 prisoners here. Today, the prison houses an estimated 2000 convicts. Otherwise, visitors and city residents head east for the water and sporting facilities of the East Coast Park. If you are interested in crocodile breeding, you can visit the Crocodile Farm or the Crocodilarium.

Crocodile Farm* and Singapore Crocodilarium*

Whether you prefer crocodiles alive or as a handbag, you can learn much about these impressive reptiles and about skinning techniques at the Crocodile Farm, 790 Upper Serangoon Road, or Singapore's Crocodilarium, 730 East Coast Parkway (both open daily 9am-5:30pm). Crocodile-skin goods are on sale at both places. For feeding times and crocodile wrestling matches at the Crocodilarium, call in advance (☎ 4473722).

East Coast Park

This recreation area on East Coast Parkway comprises 5 mi/8 km of reclaimed land with beaches and gardens plus the **Tennis Centre**

(☎ 4425966), **Parkland Golf Driving Range** (☎ 4406726), **Sailing Centre** for sailing, wind-surfing or canoeing (☎ 4495118), **Aquatic Centre** with pools and a giant waterslide, bike renting facilities and an outdoor **Food Centre.**

THE ISLANDS

Other than the main island, Singapore is comprised of 57 islets, half of which are uninhabited. Only Sentosa has been developed as a resort centre.

Sentosa

This island is much appreciated by Singaporeans who picnic here on weekends. Take a walk in the forest, rent a bike, play a game of golf at the 18-hole course, roller skate on the giant rink or go to one of the small beaches (which are, unfortunately, overcrowded). There's a 3.75 mi/6 km monorail with six stops on the island.

Attractions include the **Coralarium** and **Insectarium** (☎ 4725220), with 2500 varieties of shell and coral and 4000 insects, the **Maritime Museum,** a **Musical Fountain** (sound and light shows daily 8, 8:30 and 9pm; additional shows Sat and the eve of holidays 7:30 and 9:30pm) and the 19th-century British **Fort Siloso and Surrender Chamber** (☎ 4754045), where the history of the Japanese surrender in 1945 is presented with life-size wax figures (for further information on Sentosa Island, ☎ 2707888).

Departures to Sentosa are by ferry from the World Trade Centre every 15 minutes (Mon-Thurs 7:30am-10:45pm, Fri-Sun, holidays and the eve of holidays 7:30am-11pm). The ferry trip takes six minutes. Departures by cable car from Mount Faber or Jardine Steps (Mon-Sat 10am-7:30pm, Sun and holidays 9am-7:30pm).

Other islands

Other than Sentosa, only the islands of **Kusu** and **St John's** are accessible by ferry. Kusu is a lovely island with nice beaches, two lagoons and a **tortoise sanctuary.** There is also a **Taoist temple** (Tua Pek Kong) and a **Malay sanctuary** (Keramat). Hundreds of thousands of worshipers converge on the temple to make offerings and pray for prosperity and fertility during the ninth lunar month (Oct-Nov). St John's is a tranquil island, with nice beaches.

For a more unusual get-away experience, discover the islands by yourself in a sampan. Among the more popular getaway islands are: **Pulau Seking,** with its several hundred inhabitants living in traditional fishing villages on stilts (there's a small **mosque** at Seking), and **Pulau Hantu** or **Sisters Island** for snorkeling and skin-diving.

Ferry service from World Trade Centre to Kusu and St John's twice daily on weekdays, eight times on Sunday and holidays. The trip to Kusu takes 30 minutes, to St John's one hour. For the other islands, charter a sampan or junk from Jardine Steps or Clifford Pier.

SUGGESTED READING

Hong Kong, Macau

Burkhard, V. R. *Chinese Creeds and Customs, Vol. I, II, III* (Hong Kong: S.C.M. Post 1953, 1955, 1958).

Cameron, Nigel. *The Cultured Pearl* (Oxford University Press, 1978).

Carew, Tim. *The Fall of Hong Kong* (Pan, 1963).

Cheng, Joseph Y. *Hong Kong: In Search of a Future* (Oxford University Press, 1985).

Clavell, James. *Tai-Pan* (Atheneum, 1966).

Coates, Austin. *City of Broken Promises* (Heinemann Asia, 1977).

——. *Myself A Mandarin* (Heinemann Educational, 1975).

——. *A Macao Narrative* (Heinemann Educational, 1978).

Crisswell, Colin. *The Taipans* (Oxford University Press, 1981).

Endacott, G. B., and Hinton, A. *A Fragrant Harbour: A Short History of Hong Kong* (Greenwood, 1977).

Endacott, G. B. *A History of Hong Kong* (Oxford University Press, 1978).

——. *Hong Kong Eclipse* (Oxford University Press, 1978).

Geiger, Theodore, and Geiger, Frances M. *Tales of Two City-States: The Development Progress of Hong Kong and Singapore* (Nat'l Planning, 1979).

Guillen-Nunez, Cesar. *Macau* (Oxford University Press, 1984).

Han Suyin. *A Many Splendoured Thing* (London, 1952).

Hughes, Richard. *Foreign Devil* (André Deutsch, 1972).

——. *Borrowed Time-Borrowed Place* (André Deutsch, 1968).

Insight Guides: *Hong Kong* (Prentice Hall, 1989).

LeCarré, John. *The Honourable Schoolboy* (Hodder & Stoughton, 1977).

Mason, Richard. *The World of Suzie Wong* (Collins, 1957).

Morris, Jan. *Hong Kong* (Random House, 1988).

Osgood, Cornelius. *The Chinese: A Study of Hong Kong Community* (University of Arizona Press, 1975).

Rand, Christopher. *Hong Kong, the Island in Between* (AMS Pr., 1952).

Savidge, Joyce. *Temples Hong Kong* (Hong Kong Government, 1977).

Siu-Kai. *Law, Society & Politics in Hong Kong* (St. Martin's Press, 1984).

Wesley-Smith, Peter. *Unequal Treaty Territory, 1898-1997: China, Great Britain & Hong Kong's New Territories* (Oxford University Press, 1983).

Singapore

Barber, Noel. *Sinister Twilight: The Fall of Singapore* (Collins, 1968).

Bedlington, Stanley S. *Malaysia and Singapore: The Building of New States* (Cornell University Press, 1978).

Buckley, Charles Burton. *An Anecdotal History of Old Times in Singapore 1819-1867.* Reprint of 1902 ed. (Oxford University Press, 1984).

Collins, Maurice. *Raffles* (Day, 1968).

Insight Guides: *Singapore* (Prentice Hall, 1989).

Josey, Alex. *Singapore: Its Past, Present & Future* (Singapore: Oxford University Press, 1980).

Turnbull, C. M. *A History of Singapore 1819-1975* (Oxford University Press, 1977).

INDEX

Hong Kong

Macau